THE FUTURE ECONOMY

THE FUTURE ECONOMY

A Crypto Insider's Guide
to the Tech Dismantling
Traditional Banking

Brandon Zemp

ForbesBooks

Copyright © 2022 by Brandon Zemp.

All rights reserved. No part of this book may be used or reproduced in any manner whatsoever without prior written consent of the author, except as provided by the United States of America copyright law.

Published by ForbesBooks, Charleston, South Carolina.
Member of Advantage Media Group.

ForbesBooks is a registered trademark, and the ForbesBooks colophon is a trademark of Forbes Media, LLC.

Printed in the United States of America.

10 9 8 7 6 5 4 3 2 1

ISBN: 978-1-95588-400-6
LCCN: 2022907542

This custom publication is intended to provide accurate information and the opinions of the author in regard to the subject matter covered. It is sold with the understanding that the publisher, Advantage|ForbesBooks, is not engaged in rendering legal, financial, or professional services of any kind. If legal advice or other expert assistance is required, the reader is advised to seek the services of a competent professional.

 Advantage Media Group is proud to be a part of the Tree Neutral® program. Tree Neutral offsets the number of trees consumed in the production and printing of this book by taking proactive steps such as planting trees in direct proportion to the number of trees used to print books. To learn more about Tree Neutral, please visit **www.treeneutral.com**.

Since 1917, Forbes has remained steadfast in its mission to serve as the defining voice of entrepreneurial capitalism. ForbesBooks, launched in 2016 through a partnership with Advantage Media Group, furthers that aim by helping business and thought leaders bring their stories, passion, and knowledge to the forefront in custom books. Opinions expressed by ForbesBooks authors are their own. To be considered for publication, please visit **forbesbooks.com**.

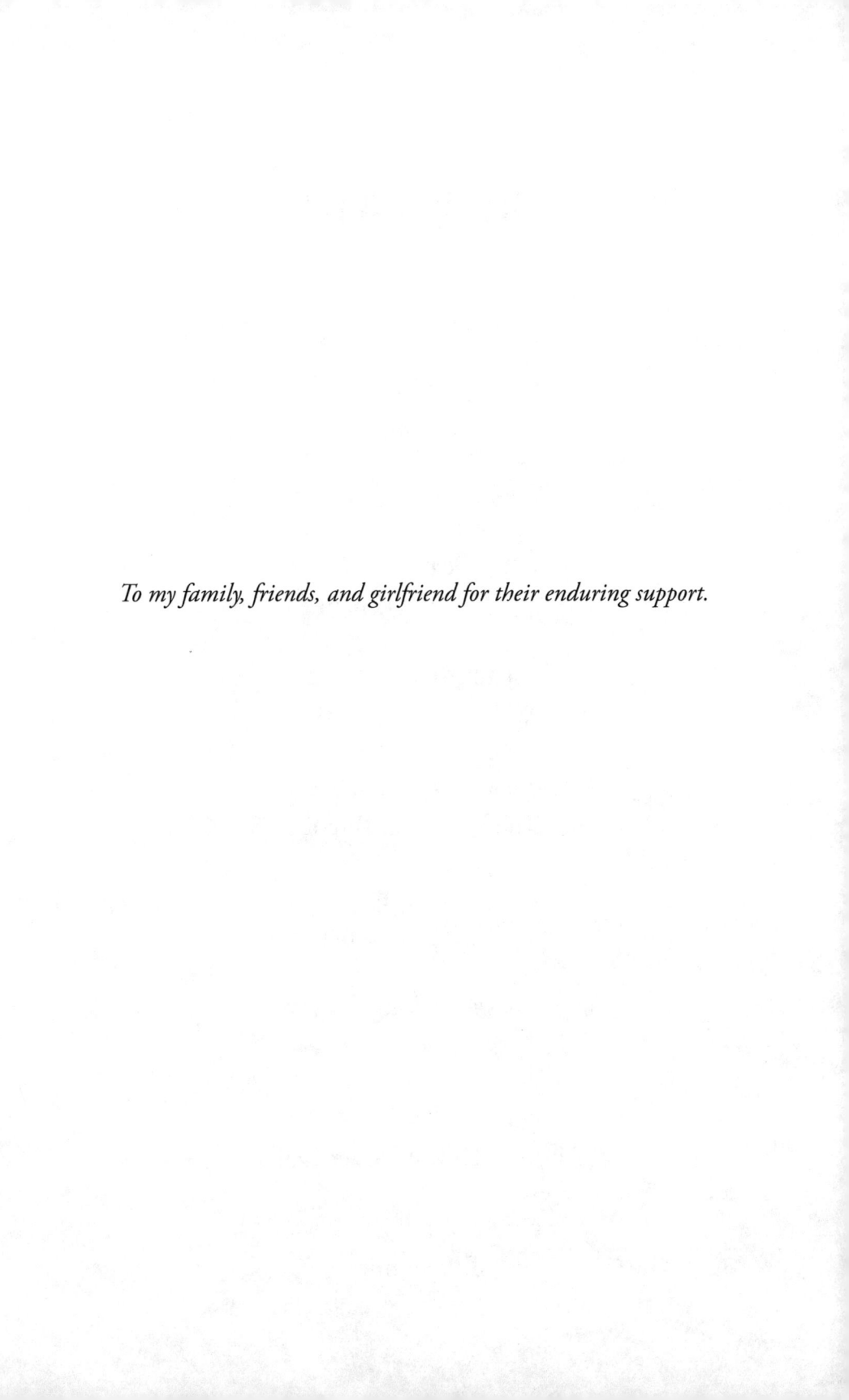

To my family, friends, and girlfriend for their enduring support.

CONTENTS

INTRODUCTION — 1

CHAPTER 1 — 6
More Free, More Fair

CHAPTER 2 — 18
Meet Blockchain

CHAPTER 3 — 28
Welcome to the Mint

CHAPTER 4 — 40
The Planet on Bitcoin

CHAPTER 5 — 52
A Crypto-Copia

CHAPTER 6 — 66
Nifty NFTs

CHAPTER 7 — 80
Another Day, Another Dollar

CHAPTER 8 — 96
Tokenomics

CHAPTER 9 — 106
DeFi Demystified

CHAPTER 10 — 122
Blockchain Unchained

CHAPTER 11 — 138
Memecoins

CHAPTER 12 — 150
Pick Your Platform

CHAPTER 13 — 160
Location, Location, Location

CHAPTER 14 — 176
Crypto Careers

CONCLUSION — 186
What's Next for Blockchain?

ACKNOWLEDGMENTS — 194

ABOUT THE AUTHOR — 196

INTRODUCTION

Cryptocurrencies and blockchain are changing the landscape of economies and trade as we know it. And we are only just beginning to scratch the surface of how they can be applied and implemented across industries.

Some crypto, like Bitcoin, is mainstream already. It is part of our pop culture. Every day we see it in the news. Nearly every major news outlet has a dedicated landing page for covering trends in Bitcoin and blockchain. The technology has been growing exponentially since its inception over a decade ago. A whole ecosystem of industries has sprung up around it.

A lot of you might be wondering, *Am I too late? Surely, the ship has sailed. The money to be made has been made, and development is well on its way without me.*

But the opposite is true. While many people have invested in Bitcoin, the technology behind it remains by and large a mystery, and the rest of the market has not reached nearly the same level of sweeping popularity, despite its extensive applications and broad potential. Case in point: The number one job in demand for college graduates is blockchain developers, and there is a shortage of degrees for computer science graduates. Everything is trending toward crypto, and there are not enough people to fill that demand. Now is the perfect time to get involved. As we will see in the next chapter, the industry has already had several booms and bubbles. It is starting to stabilize and take root.

Whether you are an investor looking to diversify your portfolio, an entrepreneur aiming to streamline logistics and increase net profits, or a student keen to get in on the ground floor creating the infrastructure for this emerging technology—crypto is going to be an integral part of the way forward. This book will take you through the past, the present, and, most importantly, the future of this space.

> **Everything is trending toward crypto, and there are not enough people to fill that demand.**

It can be confusing when you first enter the world of crypto. Not only are there a multitude of so-called altcoins out there—their applications and the ways we interact with them are hugely diverse—but also there is a whole language around blockchain that you have to learn. What is blockchain, for starters? What does it mean to "mine" cryptocurrency? Even more baffling is the fact that many cryptocurrencies do not aim to be currencies in the traditional sense at all.

Trying to find your way on your own can be just as bewildering. Mainstream media coverage often lags behind real-time developments in the market. And information gets watered down to make for better headlines or more easily digestible content for a wider audience. The chatter, the hype—this book cuts through all that to get to the meat.

It has been my mission to demystify the space and grow the community. I wanted to write this book as a tool for people who are interested but don't know where to start or how to deepen their involvement. I am extremely passionate about this technology's capacity to transform lives, and I want you to feel the same. When it comes to crypto, if you are standing at the edge of the pool, dipping your toes in, or maybe even wading in the shallows already, by the end of the book, you'll be doing Olympic-style backflips into the deep end.

I got interested in crypto and blockchain when I was still in college. But it was not until I fully committed to joining the industry that I truly started to understand its potential, not to mention see the payoffs. Since then, I have been expanding my knowledge and sharing it with others through my podcast, consulting work, blog, and other books. I launched my company, *BlockHash*, to address the dearth of information in the industry and then later started the podcast of the same name. I personally wanted to learn more and share these conversations with a wider audience.

> **Crypto is going to be an integral part of the way forward.**

The podcast has grown quite a bit, and I have not missed a single week in two years. I talk to a CEO, author, economist, founder, or innovator every week. I have had the opportunity to speak with some of the greatest minds and most creative innovators, people who are pushing the boundaries of this tech.

We actually have too many guests to feature on the podcast. One of the things I love most about the industry is how passionate everyone is. There is no shortage of interesting people working on incredible, forward-thinking projects. So these connections and interactions have given me an edge. There are very few people in the space who have done what I have done.

This book is a deep dive into that exceptionally unique perspective. I am bringing the sum total of my and my network's expertise to this book. Collectively, we have covered every possible aspect of this industry—from theory and conception to the explosion of diversity in cryptos to the skyrocketing level of interest and rapid development we see today. And as a result, *BlockHash* is consistently one of the highest-ranked podcasts on blockchain across platforms.

I have also grown as an investor. I learned to apply my lifelong interest in math and analytics to investing and trading. I quickly excelled at swing trading crypto, which is an incredibly volatile market. I was one of the first people to mine bitcoin in Oregon and begin day-trading tokens. And now I help other people do the same—from the secure purchase, trading, and storage of crypto to point-of-sale solutions for businesses to providing market analysis and breakdowns for investors. I have done all that personally and through my business with great success.

Having read a lot of books on blockchain—it is kind of my job to stay on top of things in order to be the best person to solve problems and educate people—I found that almost all of them have the same narrative: They are informative, which is great, but they are not often engaging or playful. They fail to get you excited. They don't *draw you in*. I am in a unique position to bring the crypto space to you in an engaging, fun way. I want people to get involved in this industry. I want to see the crypto community grow. So I want you to be as excited about it as I am.

We live in a digital age, and crypto is a digital technology. So why read a book—a holdover from the analog era—about it? We have strayed from reading as a primary form of communication, education, and entertainment. Many of us digital natives have never known life without an iPhone or iPad in our hands. But there is a necessity for reading. I think you have to read about something to really understand it, to sit with it and think deeply about it. You can consume countless YouTube videos on the same subject, but it won't hold a candle to what you'll learn from picking up this book and really digging down into the world of crypto and blockchain. (Not to mention, unlike YouTube, this is ad-free.)

In this book, we will explore the origins of crypto, starting with a history of blockchain and Bitcoin. We'll examine different cryptocurrencies and their applications, and lastly, we'll explore the practical considerations of working in the industry and what that can look like. I built the book around some of the most frequently asked questions from podcast listeners—the things you really want to know—as well as the topics I think are going to be the most pressing for the future of the industry. Basically, we'll look at the big questions and the nitty-gritty and go through theory and practice, leaving no stone unturned. Along the way, I will be introducing some of the amazing people I have interviewed on the podcast and their stories of the weird, wild, wonderful world of crypto.

There are so many opportunities still open for getting involved in the trading, development, and implementation of this technology. If you're looking to pursue a career in the field, build blockchain applications for your company, or simply make more informed investments in crypto, this book is an absolutely essential read. Those of you who know me, who know my podcast, know that it will be a fun ride. And those of you who don't, buckle up.

CHAPTER 1
MORE FREE, MORE FAIR

The industry was born in 2008 when Bitcoin's white paper was published, along with the creation of Bitcoin. There had been other more academic or theoretical iterations of the idea of cryptocurrency as early as the 1970s, but this was the first to be actualized and taken seriously. This revolutionary document and the technology behind it were created by the now-famous Satoshi Nakamoto. No one knows if he is a real person, dead or alive, a group or an individual. There is a lot of mythology around the origins of Bitcoin. But he, it, she, whatever created this amazing technology. Satoshi basically posited that the main issue with electronic payments was the need for trust in a third party to process the transaction, a kind of middleman between the buyer and the seller. Satoshi proposed a peer-to-peer system based on cryptographic proof as the solution, and that became the foundation for what we know today as blockchain. (I was so enthralled with the theory behind crypto that I wrote my first book, *The Satoshi Sequence*, on it.)

But at that time, like most people, my life was on a different track. I was a freshman in high school when the white paper was released and Bitcoin was created, and I knew nothing about it. Before crypto and blockchain, sports were my life—football, track, wrestling. I was born and raised in Oregon, but I dreamed of being the star quarterback for the Cowboys. By the time I got to high school, I realized that might be a stretch and decided to switch gears. I thought about going premed and becoming a doctor. I got into a good liberal arts school, Pitzer College in Claremont, California. Pitzer is part of a consortium, so I had a broad, comprehensive education. Not many people can say they took classes at five different premier universities in pursuit of a degree.

However, I discovered quickly that the path I was on was more difficult than I thought. It would mean another ten years of study—going through medical school and postgrad en route to becoming a neurosurgeon or neuroscientist. If you want to be a biology major, you take biology classes and get your degree. But if you want to do a BS in neuroscience, you have to take all the prerequisites—chemistry, biology, physics, pretty much all the sciences. It combines all the toughest classes in the major science degrees, which was an overwhelming prospect. I basically undertook a course schedule stuffed to the brim, and I was playing Division III football. I had scant free time. My life was a hamster wheel of classes, study time, football practice and games, eating, and sleeping. Rinse and repeat.

So it was a horrible lifestyle choice.

It was not until 2013, when I was a freshman in college, that Bitcoin had its first major runup in price, and I took notice—along with a lot of people who had never heard of it before. It was making some pretty splashy headlines for the first time: magical internet money that people were apparently getting rich from. A few people anyway. That year, the value of Bitcoin went from about $13 in January to a peak of over $1,100 toward the end of the year. Crazy returns on investment. Everyone wanted to learn more and get in on the ground floor. It became a cult phenomenon. How could something digital have so much value? People naturally compared it to physical and traditional assets; the phrase "digital gold" was coined.

In what very little free time I had, I took investment classes. I went to a conference in Las Vegas, attended by financial folks, and Bitcoin was on everyone's lips. The headliner was Peter Schiff, a huge goldbug and major investor in and advocate for precious metals. He is infamous for being a heel in the crypto space. He is a perennial crypto-skeptic no matter how meteorically it increases in price. Bitcoin could be worth $60,000, and he would hate it; it could be $3,000, and he would still hate it. And he hated Bitcoin back then, too. Schiff has been mostly wrong about Bitcoin's performance, but at the time, I admired him. That same year, despite Bitcoin's dramatic rise, Peter Schiff refused to acknowledge that it had any utility. Schiff was, and remains, the villain, the counterpoint to my own position. He is the guy lying on the beach when a hurricane is about to hit, wondering why he is the only one there working on his tan. He's in total denial.

But crypto can be like that, a Marmite figure: You either love it or hate. I started to love it.

That conference sparked my interest in finance in general and Bitcoin in particular. There was a lot I didn't understand when I started out. What is a digital asset? A digital store of value? (Which might be familiar questions to some of you.) I spent more time exploring and learning about it, and I discovered that Bitcoin was this unique thing—the first major innovation in our monetary system in decades, centuries even—outside of things like fiat currency, bank credit, or credit cards, which were in many ways extensions or evolutions of the existing system. One of the things that really got me excited was that the technology was not linked to or controlled by any individual, company, or nation-state. It's decentralized. It had the potential to be more free, more fair, and more secure than traditional financial tools.

So I bought a little and kept an eye on it.

Then Bitcoin was quiet for a few years. The markets cooled; the price came down to earth, to the mid- to low hundreds. I think a lot of people thought that would be the end of the experiment. It stayed like that until 2016, when it started to gain traction again. People talked more about it; the price rose. Even on my campus, I heard people discussing it casually. Campuses are like petri dishes for new tech and the next big thing. If you hear college students and faculty talking about something, it is probably a sign to pay attention. Uber, for example: College kids were all about it. Then it blew up and became the household name it is today.

By 2016, new tokens were coming into play. A market was maturing, coming into its own. Litecoin, Ripple, Dash, Monero stepped onto the scene—as did new projects, like Ethereum, that were looking beyond the financial aspect. They began leveraging the technology for other interests—contracts, proof of work or payment, shipping, even things like voting. But we'll get into all that later.

I finished my four years of college, ground it out, and got the degree. I had to go through that to understand that I did not want to be in that field forever. I realized I would end up doing the same grueling, monotonous hard work that would leave me with zero time to, well, *live*. Not to mention the kind of debt I would have to take on to do it. Basically, it would suck.

So when I graduated in 2017, I had doubts about what to do going forward. I knew what I did *not* want to do, and that was how I ended up changing course and getting into crypto and blockchain. I was curious how this technology would shape the industry, the market, the future. And I wasn't alone. There was an abundance of curiosity in and around the space. More tokens were popping up, and existing ones were maturing and evolving. I started to wonder, "Could this really turn into a major global market or even revolutionize the way we live day to day?"

That year also saw a booming bull market; Bitcoin peaked in the fourth quarter, from under $1,000 earlier that year to around $20,000 near year's end. Other cryptocurrencies also shot up in price, many with bigger returns than Bitcoin. Ethereum went from under $10 to just over $1,000 in the same period. It was a wild time in the trading scene. I was practically glued to my laptop. I had invested in Ethereum and made a bunch of money, which confirmed my decision to change course from neuroscience and the med school track to cryptocurrency. The industry was coming into fruition. I began to travel and meet with industry experts and innovators. I traveled through parts of Europe and North and South America learning about all the different ways people were implementing this technology. That led me to publish my first book, *The Satoshi Sequence*, which was a kind of personal manifesto articulating my ideas on the space.

So the market had this massive runup, sparking frenzied global interest seemingly out of nowhere. The market crashed, but by 2018, I knew I had made the right choice of industry.

Then the COVID-19 pandemic hit in 2020. We saw the biggest drop in economic output since the Depression. Whole industries ground to a halt. There were supply shortages and panic buying. More and more people started working from home and finding digital solutions to the age-old problem of disease. It was truly a year for the history books. But Bitcoin followed a different trajectory from the majority of markets. It was seen as a hedge against currency devalued by massive government bailouts, stimulus payments, and expansion of social welfare in response to the pandemic. It hit a high of around

$28,000 in December and kept on rising, peaking in February 2021 at over $60,000.

People have drawn comparisons to the technology boom of the 1990s and the early days of the internet. People realize crypto is a real market that is here to stay, but it will be a bumpy road transitioning to the new technology—just like the early internet, which took a while to become integrated into the mainstream. It took time to build out infrastructure around the technology. Some of you will remember old dial-up systems to connect to the internet, waiting for pages to load, and getting dropped when your mom needed to make a call, which was on the same home phone line as the computer. But early visionaries and innovators persisted because of how much potential it had to change every aspect of daily life. And the technology became easier to use, faster, more accessible, and more efficient. Now we're looking at things like 5G, quantum encryption, and Web 3.0.

It's the same with crypto. It will take time to build out infrastructure to allow for more efficient trading, investing, and other applications. And it will require people to develop and build that infrastructure. It is just as important that the crypto community grow along with technology.

Another facet of the early internet were bubbles and crashes. The dot-com bubble is a primary example. Companies that were flying high are nonexistent now. And other companies (think Amazon, Microsoft, Apple) born out of that era grew to create incredible things that still dominate the market space and that we cannot imagine our lives without.

> **People realize crypto is a real market that is here to stay, but it will be a bumpy road transitioning to the new technology.**

And again crypto is the same: So many start-ups and projects have matured since 2017 (and others have largely disappeared from the market, like Namesake). In the five years since then, the space has grown exponentially. Coinbase, for example, has become the largest cryptocurrency exchange in the US. In fact, it has been so successful that getting a cryptocurrency listed on the exchange plays such a huge role in its acceptance, it is referred to as the Coinbase effect. Gemini, Binance, and other established exchanges have risen to prominence. There are stablecoins like Tether, the value of which is tied directly to the US dollar. These developments would have been unimaginable ten or fifteen years ago. The technology is advancing so rapidly that regulation has not always managed to keep up.

And traditional investment groups, banks, and hedge funds are jumping in on the action, to the tune of billions of dollars. Icons like Elon Musk are throwing their hat in and figuring out how to adapt blockchain technology. Celebrities like Snoop Dogg, Paris Hilton, and Gene Simmons are promoting it. Amazon and PayPal are incorporating it into their payment systems. Even governments are starting to build on the technology (some more fervently or successfully than others).

At the same time, we are in the early adoption stage. Everyone knows what Bitcoin is—even boomers—and many are aware of the other cryptocurrencies or altcoins. Many people own bitcoin, but that is not how we should gauge its success, much less its potential. There are still relatively few people invested in the rest of crypto as a market. People have bought bitcoin and even other altcoins because they are a speculative vehicle and the hottest thing in finance, but few casual investors understand the market or really try to *engage* with the space. They do not appreciate how crypto will revolutionize finance or how the market will grow so much it disrupts traditional financial markets. Each day people are debating whether Bitcoin is a better monetary standard than gold. They are debating every day how to use blockchain to solve real-world issues. That's because there are so many launching pads for blockchain as a technology for different industries.

So whether or not people own bitcoin is not the best metric to use as a measure of engagement with or interest in the industry. More important is the number of people interested in building the infrastructure and broadening the applications of blockchain technology. And I'm guessing since you're reading this book, you are one of those people.

For my own part, since making the pivot to crypto, I have been able to adopt a more relaxed, fulfilling lifestyle. I still work hard—don't get me wrong—but I have been able to shape my life into what I want it to be. I live in Medellín, Colombia, a dynamic city that has attracted many other entrepreneurs, technologists, and people in the start-up scene. I spend my days producing the podcast, learning about new trends in the industry, educating others, helping people through my consulting business, and managing a portfolio of crypto investments. I love what I do and the freedom it has given me.

So where is the industry headed, and what can joining the crypto community look like for you? It is a flexible technology, so there are so many industries that blockchain will become an integral part of. It can be applied to almost anything. We have only just skimmed the surface of what can actually be done at scale. One thing I have learned through hosting the podcast is that the opportunities truly are limitless—and more importantly, they are still open to anyone wanting to answer the call.

Finance, obviously, will be overhauled. Blockchain changes how we handle money, make loans, and send money to each other. It is creating financial on-ramps for people who do not traditionally have access to start-up funds or pools of money, people who are impoverished or live in places without access to credit, loans, credit scores, debit cards, and other financial instruments. One of the biggest use cases is creating financial openness, opportunity, and diversity.

But blockchain can accomplish so many things beyond simple finance. Take smart contracts (which we'll get into later). Imagine being able to eliminate third parties or middlemen when doing business, whether B2B (business to business) or B2C (business to customer) work, or even as an individual when you make a contract with an insurance company, a contractor, or your landlord, for example. It will allow people to decentralize contacts—dealing only with one other party, not an outside party. It is simply more efficient. It cuts fees and simplifies logistics. It's easier, cheaper, faster, and more efficient. It is good for business when you are at scale, and every minor change makes the difference between a million dollars saved or lost. It has the potential to create tremendous wealth from a logistics point of view.

> **Blockchain can accomplish so many things beyond simple finance.**

Beyond that, blockchain can help with record keeping, which means there are applications in transportation, healthcare, and government. You can prove that a birth certificate is authentic or that a legal document is genuine without going through the drudgery of bureaucratic red tape. Even more mundane things like storing and sending your iPhone photos can be done through blockchain. The technology works with literally any digital asset. And not only does blockchain ensure secure transactions, but transactions can also be made anonymously.

It is more than just speculation and making money. Price action and market value might be what get you interested. But there is much more than the hard numbers and the money you can make. It is an industry that is changing lives, that is creating products and services, and that has a bright future. We should not fixate so much on the dollar value as on what it can do for reshaping the landscape of our lives for the better. Getting involved does not just mean investing.

Yeah, you can quintuple, 10x, 100x your money. But this technology is changing society. And maybe you should join the revolution.

There is a lot to cover. Coming up, we will be taking a closer look at the most recent developments in the industry in order to better understand what lies ahead. This will include discussions of Bitcoin and other cryptocurrencies, NFTs and centralized cryptos, decentralized finance, nonfinancial blockchain applications, and a guide to working in the industry. But before we get to any of that, let's examine the technologies behind Web 3.0. We'll get into how they work, where they come from, and where they're going. In chapter 2, we'll take a crash course on blockchain. This will give you a strong foundation for understanding the basics of the technology and set you up for learning about the finer points of blockchain as we move ahead.

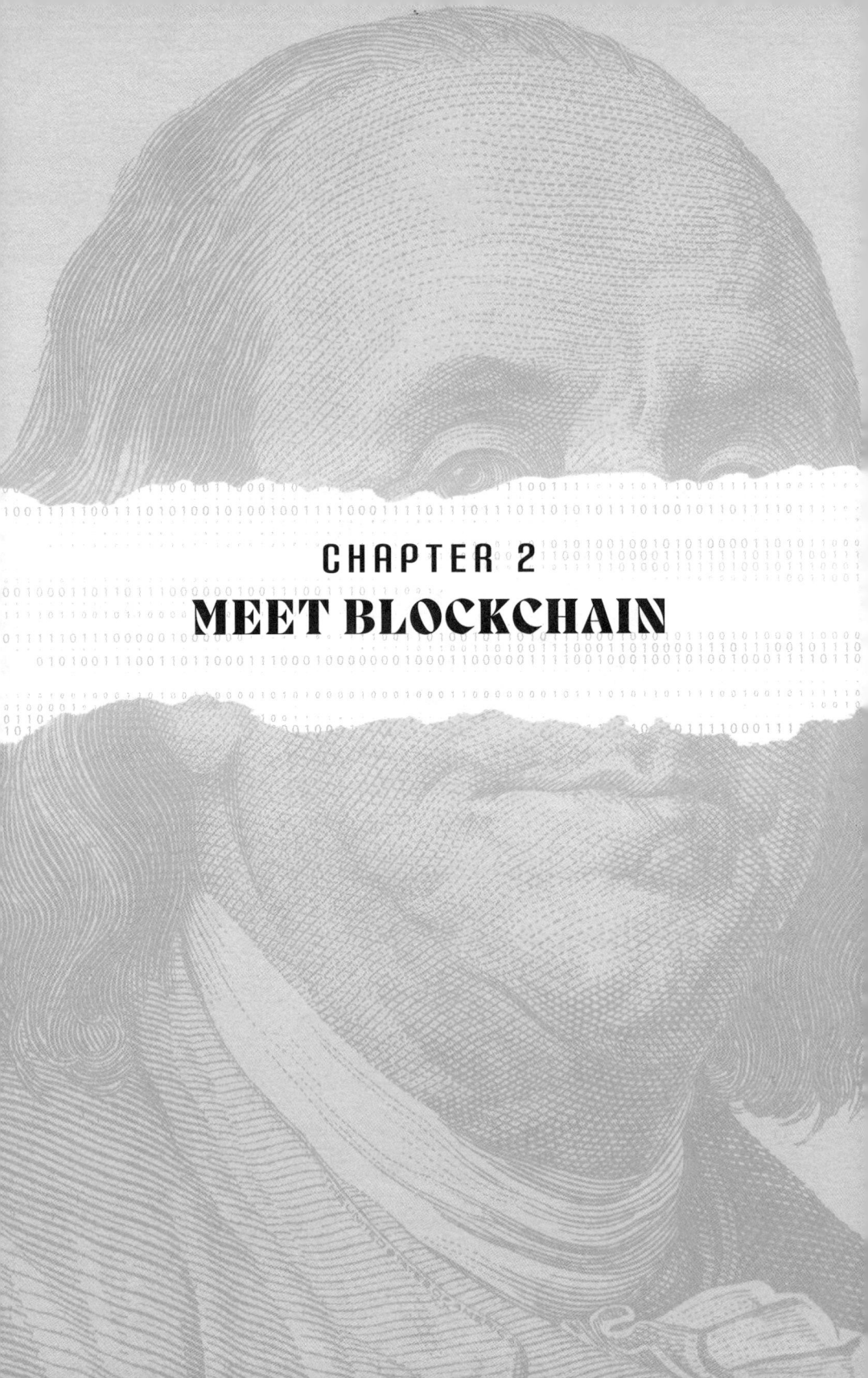

CHAPTER 2
MEET BLOCKCHAIN

One of the stumbling blocks for people who want to get involved in blockchain is getting their head around the concept to begin with. To put it in the simplest possible terms, blockchain is a digital ledger of transactions distributed across a network of computers, which means it is decentralized and transparent. Each block in the blockchain contains a number of transactions. With each new transaction, a record of that transaction is added to the ledger. That decentralized database—that blockchain—is also known as distributed ledger technology. You can picture it like a digital version of Legoland.

The best way to think of it is as a network of computers, similar to the internet except there are no central points where all the data is stored. The blockchain data is stored and copied on every computer or node in the network all over the world by whoever chooses to run a computer or node, which means the data is not controlled by a single group, party, or entity. Every node on the network can be operated by anyone. These days it is as easy as buying a machine or even using your laptop or phone to run a node. If you download a bitcoin wallet, you're probably running a bitcoin node without having to do anything to actively, or even knowingly, support the network.

In addition to being decentralized, an important facet of the technology is the fact that it is secure. Every block of transactions is cryptographically secured through what is called a hash, which is a string of numbers and letters. I sometimes picture this like the scenes in *The Imitation Game* when they show the enigma machines designed by Alan Turing—but a much faster, much more secure twenty-first-century version. Each unique hash can only be decrypted with a private key, or seed, provided by the person sending something via blockchain that has that hash attached to it. Now this may sound a little complicated, but at the most basic conceptual level, it is no different from buying a car or house and getting the unique set of keys to it along with your purchase. Only you can't take a hash down to your local Home Depot and ask for a copy.

So that is the foundation, the jumping-off point. But I want to focus on what you can *do* with the technology rather than getting bogged down in the very complicated minutiae, mathematics, and technical jargon of how it works.

Laying the Foundations for Blockchain

Another thing that can make people hesitant when they start out in the industry is the idea that blockchain is too new, which may make people think that it is therefore too volatile or unpredictable, or maybe it will just disappear from the technoscape, like laser discs or Google glasses. But as in so many instances, knowing our history can put those fears to bed. There are a number of precursors to blockchain. A lot of little technologies that preceded blockchain helped enable its emergence, even though blockchain itself is a novel technology.

Elements of the technology have been in use for decades. Things like PGP encryption and VPNs are similar in some ways. They are decentralized and secure, much like blockchain.

Pretty Good Privacy (PGP), also known as Person to Person (P2P), ensures only the person on the receiving end of a communication has the key to open the files through encryption and authentication. In the case of PGP email, it only goes from point A to point B. There is no intermediary or centralized database. If you are worried about the Google overlords reading your email, or someone has your password and you have privacy concerns, or a government agency is spying on you, or perhaps you are a government agent who has to protect your data from spies, then cutting out the middleman is a great way to reduce your risk of exposure.

Blockchain works in a comparable way when you send a transaction. For example, if I send you bitcoin, it will go directly from me to you. It will not go through an institution, third party, or random node.

Virtual private networks (VPNs) also function in an analogous fashion. You can use a node in a different country to change your IP address to access information. It is a decentralized system that opens your access to avoid being surveilled, monitored, or blocked. Because VPNs operate across a decentralized network, you can access different parts of the internet that may otherwise be blocked in your local area.

For example, if you are in the UK and you want to binge-watch a show on Netflix that only appears on the US site, you can use a VPN to connect to a different node, which changes your IP address and allows you to access the US-based network and stream that show. Or when the stakes are higher, say, if you are in China and want to learn about events or topics blocked or monitored by China's firewall—

Tiananmen Square or the persecution of Uyghurs in Xinjiang—you can use a VPN to do that, too.

Essentially these technologies encode data using a hashing algorithm to scramble the data, which can only be reassembled with a private key. While PGP and VPNs are not exactly the same on the whole as blockchain, elements of those technologies have been incorporated into blockchain technology. Blockchain uses the process of encoding data through hashes, which lends security to the network because no one can easily decrypt, steal, or intercept it.

The Byzantine Generals Problem

So what makes blockchain different from its predecessors? Why is it such a game changer? The thing with blockchain is that it is the first time a network has been able to solve the Byzantine Fault Problem, also commonly known as the Byzantine Generals Problem. The problem is essentially this: Imagine you are in a battle and have an army attacking on two or more fronts; the enemy is strong enough to defend itself from one attacking army at a time but not two or more simultaneously. All parties must agree on a strategy and act in concert—otherwise your army will face complete failure and defeat. To add to the complexity, there may be officers, messengers, or other actors who are unreliable or corrupt working to undermine your victory. So how do you coordinate your soldiers to attack or retreat as

> **Blockchain uses the process of encoding data through hashes, which lends security to the network because no one can easily decrypt, steal, or intercept it.**

one? If you are in multiple locations involving multiple decision-making processes and multiple actors, how do you reach consensus on what to do and execute that decision at the same time?

While it is an interesting thought experiment, it is also a common real-world problem in many facets of society, including the internet. Blockchain creates consensus over the internet with transactions. Bitcoin was the first to accomplish this and the first to prove that the Byzantine Generals Problem could be solved. The solution was blockchain. For example, there are millions of people using Bitcoin. I want to send some bitcoin to you, but how does everyone else know I am making that transaction? In a decentralized network, how does the *market* know? How do others verify that the transaction was completed? That conundrum has real-world repercussions. But blockchain confirms transactions with many different nodes, which are then propagated as transactions across the network. It creates a permanent public record, so to speak. If we go back to the battle analogy, it might look like a movie scene set in the Cold War era where two soldiers have to turn their keys at the exact same moment to activate a nuclear launch.

It might sound like an obvious solution, but it revolutionizes the internet. It takes the internet as it is today and adapts it to a completely digital world.

So What's New about Blockchain?

More and more of our everyday activity is taking place online. We have entered the age of the Internet of Things, wherein all devices are connected. We are sharing our lives and connecting online through social media, gaming, and other forums. We conduct our businesses, manage bank accounts, make purchases, and do a whole host of other things all online.

Blockchain opens up even more opportunities to do things online but with one clear distinction: *to have control over them.*

Let's say you set up an Instagram account. You have ownership and control of your account—you can post whatever you like for the most part—but ultimately it's not *owned* by you. The account is owned by the company. With blockchain/Web 3.0, you can create your own version of an Instagram account that no one can shut down or moderate. You can post anything, monetize it how you wish, take it with you anywhere (digitally or in the real world), and it connects to just about everything frictionlessly.

Or say you want to sign into a website. The website might let you connect your Google profile or log in via Google, which a lot of people do mainly because it means not having to enter or remember different passwords for every site you visit. Facebook or Instagram gets used that way, too. Moreover, those apps are how people identify you online; they visit your social media profiles and get to know you. But what if you had a single digital identity that could go anywhere with you online, to prove and verify who you are? You could use it to instantly connect to or talk privately with people. If you have full control over your own digital profile or identity, you can leverage that in any way you choose. And you can do that—you can create a digital identity for yourself with blockchain. Think of it like a digital passport. If I wanted to create an integration or connect with someone else or another business, I could do it without restriction or friction using blockchain.

> **Blockchain opens up even more opportunities to do things online but with one clear distinction:** *to have control over them.*

Or let's say you are attending a digital concert or festival, like a virtual Coachella. Having a digital identity means you could hold all your tickets digitally, pay for in-game merchandise, and verify you have that money—without having to use a third party like a bank.

Blockchain offers total validation for anything digital—a kind of digital integrity and authentication that never really existed before. We'll get into more real-world applications later on.

What Can You *Do* with Blockchain?

If you're a coder or developer, you can create a blockchain. New blockchains are created every day, in fact. The challenge is to create one that is efficient, cost-effective, scalable to millions if not billions of users and transactions, secure, private—basically whatever your end user wants.

Enter Vitalik Buterin. He is one of the most important people in the crypto space. By all accounts, he is rather aloof—a geeky, coder type of guy. (As opposed to a front and center, in the spotlight, Elon Musk type.) He is incredibly intelligent, an innovator, and he has a great deal of influence. He's highly respected and regarded, and his opinion holds a ton of weight.

Vitalik and a few other collaborators saw what Bitcoin was able to do, looked at the underlying technology that made it possible, and asked, "How can this decentralized, distributed network fulfill other uses?" Eventually they created Ethereum.

Ethereum uses open-source blockchain technology to create other things that are decentralized, such as smart contracts. These are essentially self-executing contracts that do not require an entity to fulfill them. With a smart contract, you can do all kinds of things. It means you can eliminate a middleman. A smart contract establishes an agreement between party A and party B. For example, if you were to purchase real estate, you would normally need a broker. But using blockchain, you no longer need that broker to help navigate the legal and financial practices of the industry—in particular, the transferal of ownership. As long as sender and receiver, person A and person B, are in agreement, then the contract can be executed without interference (or fees) from third parties.

Smart contracts can also be used to create tokens (cryptocurrencies)—and there are countless things to do with tokens—but a contract can govern the economics behind a token. For example, it can be applied to a release schedule: If you want to mint a million tokens, a smart contract can auto-fulfill the release in different payment cycles—ten monthly releases of one hundred thousand tokens, for instance. Or it can be set up like a treasury so that it only releases when certain criteria are fulfilled by a specific party or multiple parties. Alternatively, you can use it like escrow, so funds sit in a wallet in blockchain managed by that contract.

Ethereum was the first investment I made in the crypto space, and it was the first blockchain I really engaged with by minting a token and buying something with ether (the native cryptocurrency of Ethereum). My first interaction with the Ethereum network was when I bought virtual land and virtual art on its blockchain. It made me realize that blockchain meant more than just buying cryptocurrencies. There are assets *inside* the network. Built atop Ethereum on the network are thousands of different tokens—digital assets that have given rise to massive markets. Four or five years ago it was very small. Today those markets are bigger than most competing markets.

We will be looking in depth at some of Ethereum's other projects and applications later in the book, like decentralized finance (DeFi), yields and staking platforms, and non-fungible tokens (NFTs). But for now, let's just say that Vitalik and the rest of the Ethereum Foundation created a project that is so big, so groundbreaking, a project that is supposed to bring ideas and people to consensus, but they cannot seem to come to consensus on everything. They have been trying to create Ethereum 2.0 for years—it was supposed to be up and running by now—but the network is lagging because everyone has so many ideas and opinions that they can't agree on what to do. With a decentralized network, you need people to agree before you make changes to rules that underpin the network and how it operates. You cannot just upload a quick fix or release a patch. And, well, it can be hard to get people to agree—though this applies to changes in the hardcoding of the network, not to the process by which transactions are verified within the existing system.

Which brings us back to what makes blockchain technology so unique. Yes, blockchain creates consensus over the internet, and Bitcoin was the first do it—the first to solve the Byzantine Generals Problem. And as the first application of blockchain technology and still the most successful cryptocurrency in the world today, it is important that we understand Bitcoin in particular. Next up, I will take you on a crash course of Bitcoin so that we can fully appreciate what it is, what it does, and all the doors it opened for what has come after it.

CHAPTER 3
WELCOME TO THE MINT

Bitcoin was the first real-world application of blockchain technology and the first cryptocurrency, and it remains the number one leader in the crypto market. So it is important to have a solid understanding of Bitcoin before we move into the larger world of crypto and blockchain.

Bitcoin Origins

As we discussed in chapter 1, Satoshi Nakamoto wrote the white paper on Bitcoin. No one knows who he is, nor has anyone had any correspondence with him that we know of since he launched Bitcoin. He remains one of the most important figures in the space, and yet no one has ever met him. There is a lot of speculation, some of it is pretty entertaining. There are people who think Satoshi is actually Elon Musk. Other people suspect that the CIA is behind the creation of Bitcoin. Or the Russians or Chinese. Maybe it is just the gods raining down bitcoins from above. It is fun to theorize, and I think it is part of the appeal of Bitcoin as an antigovernment, antibanking, antiestablishment, anticentralization paradigm.

It is fitting that Bitcoin, which was the catalyst for the whole industry, does not have anyone to stand behind it as the public founder. It lends a lot of mystery to the crypto space. And personally, I think it is good he does not exist as a public figure for Bitcoin, since the whole point is that it is a financial instrument for everyone, for the people. His absence reinforces the ethos of decentralization that is so essential to the technology. It is symbolic of the way Bitcoin gives back your sovereignty when it comes to money. The financial system traps many people in debt, and financial tools are not available to large swathes of the population across the world. A lot of people are stuck in a system that does not serve them and their financial interests. So people see Bitcoin as a way out. It is very democratic in that way.

Bitcoin entered the scene in 2008 when Satoshi released his white paper. That was the year the US and the world plunged into recession. Banks were engaged in risky lending practices, a real estate bubble popped, banks were lavished with massive bailouts, and people in general were skeptical of the banking and monetary systems. Satoshi alluded to wanting to create a reliable form of money that would be an alternative to the modern-day banking system and fiat currency. So the Great Recession and Bitcoin's origins are part of the same story. It is possible the recession even inspired Bitcoin's creation. We don't know.

In 2009, a few months after the white paper was published, the network was officially launched, and the first transaction was made. To begin with, it was worth practically nothing. It was more or less just a use case that a decentralized payment system could be created, one that wasn't controlled, that was immutable, and that could not be seized or manipulated. It was more than anything simply an idea, a nebulous solution to a long-standing thought experiment. Frankly, it was an underwhelming first act for a technology that was about to revolutionize nearly every aspect of our lives.

By now everyone has heard the stories of people who randomly bought thousands of bitcoins for pennies and are now millionaires. There is the infamous pizza story: a Florida man paid ten thousand bitcoins for two pizzas in the first ever bitcoin transaction. Today, that would be valued at nearly $500 million—for two pizzas. And there are many more tales of people who lost their trove of bitcoins or simply forgot about it. Those were the first adopters.

It was not until Bitcoin first spiked up in value between 2009 and 2013, when it reached $1,200—and a lot of people made a lot of money in a short period of time—that it started getting coverage on the news and people began asking, "What is this magic internet money we can't touch, hold, or physically possess but that has value?" And people started asking questions about money itself—what it does, what it could be, whom it serves. People were starting to consider Bitcoin seriously as an investment.

My own curiosity was piqued when I attended that conference in Las Vegas. The only thing people wanted to talk about was Bitcoin. How could something digital be worth so much when not long ago it was worth pennies? It was hard to grasp, even for its devotees. For me, too.

Then, between 2013 and 2017, there was a lot of experimentation with Bitcoin. Start-ups were created. Investment and speculation increased. The elevated interest nudged the price up again. People started asking what *else* you could do with Bitcoin and blockchain, which gave rise to other projects that are still around today (like Ripple, Dogecoin, and Ethereum). Are there alternatives to Bitcoin? Can you create similar tokens? Can you create a market and trade cryptos?

So, by 2017, people started piling in and investing when they saw that cryptocurrency—Bitcoin in particular—worked well as a form of money. Today Bitcoin is criticized for being slow, expensive, and generally inefficient, but it has never wavered: It has never gone offline, never been broken or hacked, and never had major issues threatening its network. It has been by and large a stable entity people could trust. And, in 2017, Bitcoin saw an incredible rise in value, running up from about $370 in 2016 to about $20,000 by the end of the year in 2017. That really opened people's eyes.

Innovation and Value

So some of the big questions about Bitcoin are: Is it a viable asset? What gives it value?

No one had seen a digital form of an asset. Gold, real estate, commodities, stocks—these all have a real-world analog. Bitcoin was fully digital—and out of everyone's control. So it truly was novel. It was a major milestone not just for investors but also for humanity, as we began to question what money could be, what an asset could be. And in a rapidly growing and changing digital world, that is so crucial.

Another takeaway I think is important about Bitcoin is that I personally see it as the first technological innovation in money we have had in thousands of years. I don't count fiat as innovative, even with digital wallets on our phones, credit cards, etc. Those aren't innovations; they're just mediums of payment. Different iterations of the same thing. Fiat—money backed by the issuing government rather than by physical commodities—is merely banknotes to supplement as an IOU. In some respects, it is merely an inflated version of government-controlled currency, which largely makes our lives more difficult over time.

In contrast, for me, Bitcoin is a technical innovation on money, on gold, that is long overdue. Especially in this digital age when nearly everything is online. You need something digital in the form of money that is "solid" like gold is but that has the flexibility of digital technology. Gold is imperfect money. It is not *made* to be money—though we have come to accept this pretty shiny rock as having value.

Value aligns perfectly when it aligns between intrinsic and subjective value. Intrinsically, Bitcoin was created to be money; subjectively, we see it as money. That makes it superior. Bitcoin is a paradigm shift.

Compare it to transportation. We used to use horses to get around. They worked. But intrinsically, a horse is an animal and not evolved to be transportation for humans. We just decided that horses are for transport. We improved upon it by inventing the car, which is both intrinsically and subjectively built for transportation. The improvement upon the horse.

So let's leave the horse behind.

From 2017 to early spring 2020, there was further development. When COVID-19 emerged, people panicked. Everything was going to hell. It felt for many like the apocalypse was dawning, and we would all be zombies by year's end. When the shit hit the fan, people did not want their money in banks or the stock market. The memory of the 2008 recession and all the personal financial losses of that event still loomed large. During the pandemic, people were stuck at home and scared, and they did what they thought would protect their families. In response, people bought toilet paper, hand sanitizer, gold—and Bitcoin.

Right after the stock market crash that ran from February to April 2020, the price of Bitcoin started going up steadily and has, for the most part, been steadily rising since then.

As a result of COVID-19 and its fallout, more people began to compare gold with Bitcoin as a store of value during the mass panic, global shutdowns, and disruptions to the supply chain. It was seen as a guard against the possible currency devaluation stemming from trillions of dollars paid out in COVID-19 stimulus payments from governments and central banks around the world. Unlike government currencies that can be printed at will, only twenty-one million bitcoins can ever be created according to its own hard-coded limits. It is a kind of immutable protection against debasement and inflation. Ironically, people even put their stimulus checks into bitcoin and earned a handsome return on their investment—much better than spending it on toilet paper, pasta, and canned food. It was another milestone.

Since then, Bitcoin has gone up tremendously, pulling the whole crypto market up with it. Meanwhile, various companies have been developing solutions with blockchain, even to combat the coronavirus itself. Doing things remotely and online during various stay-at-home and quarantine measures has raised other questions. What is the best medium for payment? How do you conduct business or manage a supply chain when you are stuck at home? Blockchain has offered some promising solutions.

As of this writing, one bitcoin is worth about $50,000. In comparison, the second leading cryptocurrency, ether, is valued at about $3,900 per token. These figures are likely to have changed dramatically by the time you read this, but the point is that its value, measured in dollars, continues its white-hot ascendancy. It's an interesting moment when an increasing number of people are starting to believe in Bitcoin as something that will preserve their money over time. People are validating through investment the fact that Bitcoin has emerged as a competitor to gold, which has been a store of value for thousands of years—ostensibly *the* store of value for much of modern human history. It is a true breakthrough moment in finance. I think we should appreciate how far we have come.

Bitcoin is a trillion-dollar digital asset that has only been around for eleven years, which is crazy. Why is it worth so much? And where is it going?

These are hard questions to answer. One reason Bitcoin is still the top dog among thousands of tokens is that in the last decade it has been the best performing asset, investment-wise, which affords it credibility. Many long-term investors, including corporations and institutions, have committed a lot of capital to Bitcoin in the expectation of a future return. There have been several landmark transactions valued at over a billion dollars.

But I think the number one reason nothing has surpassed it, even if it is not technically the "best" crypto, is its symbolism and what it means to people. It represents financial freedom, not in the way Robert Kiyosaki talks about—having enough money to retire—but being financially free from censorship; from a system that controls your money, puts you in debt, tells you what you can and cannot do; and a financial system that is ultimately unstable. For example, holding all your money in USD is a bad idea; it is losing value each day to inflation. As a result of recessions, bailouts, and quantitative easing, the money supply has burgeoned.

Bitcoin offers a better financial alternative. Money makes the world go round, but very little innovation has happened to it for a long time. Bitcoin is the next step in the evolution of money.

It is also the oldest of the cryptocurrencies and consequently has the longest track record. There are other tokens that have been around nearly as long, but they are being surpassed by new projects and competitors and do not even register in the top one hundred cryptos. So it is interesting that Bitcoin has

> **Bitcoin is the next step in the evolution of money.**

maintained that number one spot. It is simply on a whole different level when it comes to what people see as money and assets.

Bitcoin is our fearless leader in the blockchain space, the GOAT of crypto.

Regulatory Issues

Along with all the increased speculation has come increased regulation. Like any new technology, when Bitcoin was introduced in 2009, it was subject to existing regulations—or, more accurately, people using the Bitcoin network were subject to existing regulations. (The technology is essentially a protocol, which can be expressed in writing and therefore is protected under the First Amendment; likewise, because the network is decentralized, it would be nearly impossible to regulate it in the traditional sense.) But basically, because it is decentralized, it is up to each government to decide whether and how to regulate Bitcoin. Some have chosen to ban it altogether, although enforcing such bans is increasingly difficult thanks to technology that helps users circumvent online censorship, like VPNs. But most Western countries have instead periodically issued guidance on how it is to be taxed and exchanged.

> Bitcoin is our fearless leader in the blockchain space, the GOAT of crypto.

For example, in the US, legally you can use bitcoin to pay for goods and services and mine bitcoin, but you have to report profits earned from trading bitcoin if you exchange it for regular currency. And in 2013, the Financial Crimes Enforcement Network began requiring Bitcoin exchange platforms to report large exchanges and suspicious activity and collect data on their customers, much like traditional financial institutions must do. The Internal Revenue Service followed suit and issued guidance in 2014 and 2019, trying to keep up with the changes in how people invest in and use Bitcoin and the exponential growth in the number of people engaged with the network.

More Benefits of Bitcoin

Despite all this growth, there's no one to give credit to. We don't know who Satoshi is, where he or she or they might be, or if he is even alive. Who do we hand the Nobel Prize to? And what exactly *is* the technology he created?

As we have discussed generally regarding blockchain technology, Bitcoin is a peer-to-peer network. Anyone can run a node or server for Bitcoin. Anyone can participate. It is not confined to one person, company, or government. Consequently, it can't really be shut down, manipulated, or censored, and the more people who are involved, the safer and more stable the network becomes.

This means everyone has access to it. You can't shut people out. It is mostly—but not fully—anonymous. The blockchain ledger is, after all, a public record. Of course, you have to know who owns which address to know who the recipient and sender are to glean personally identifying information from the random string of characters that comprise a Bitcoin address. Other tokens are more private. But Bitcoin still gives you some of that freedom. As such, Bitcoin is also useful as a public record, which can be beneficial for companies, investors, and taxpayers when it comes to accounting and reporting. It provides a good balance between anonymity and transparency.

People have debated if it's possible to hack Bitcoin. For example, can a single block on the blockchain be hacked? But no one has ever hacked the SHA-256 hash, which is the hashing algorithm used by Bitcoin (among many other functions unrelated to crypto) and was originally designed by the US National Security Agency. It would basically require a supercomputer to do so, and you would have to hack every block that has ever been put on the Bitcoin network—and new blocks are added every day—which would take an unfathomable number of years. Basically, it is mathematically impossible. So it is an unhackable network. A skilled hacker can bring down Twitter, Instagram, or the Visa payment system for a day. But Bitcoin? Forget it.

Mining is another important part of Bitcoin technology—and it can be confusing for many people starting out. Essentially what it means is that in order for transactions to be put into a block on the Bitcoin network, you need a "miner" to facilitate that transaction. I used to be a miner. In fact, I had a warehouse with hundreds of miners. It is more complicated than most people think, although theoretically anyone could do it. Five or six years ago, there were not yet machines that were plug and play, that could readily mine bitcoin right away. You had to build it out, code the software, invest in expensive graphics cards, configure the computer, and so forth before you could begin mining. Now you can buy an ASIC miner, plug it in, log in, and start mining.

When you set up one of these mining machines, it competes with other machines to solve sets of highly complex, arbitrary math problems, which are at the heart of Bitcoin's cryptographic function. When you solve one of these math problems ahead of everyone else, you can place a block on the blockchain. So people lend their computing power to the network to facilitate those transactions, and they are awarded with a little bit of bitcoin in return. It is a built-in economic model for Bitcoin to reward and incentivize people to participate in the network.

There is a huge market for mining unto itself, but it is not necessarily something I recommend anyone dive into because it requires a lot of money up front and technical know-how to be profitable. The thing to understand is that mining affects Bitcoin as an asset, its price, and trading. We will talk more about mining later on, including questions about its profitability, environmental impact, and alternatives to mining.

We have looked at Bitcoin's past and present. Coming up we'll have a go at Bitcoin's future. As promised, we will explore its environmental impact, the viability of mining bitcoin, and the growing market of other tokens and how they might affect Bitcoin's success.

CHAPTER 4
THE PLANET ON BITCOIN

People know that Bitcoin uses a lot of energy, and it consistently increases its energy consumption each year. The more people who use it, transact with it, mine with it, and participate in the proof of work consensus method, the more energy is required because at its heart, proof of work is really just proof that you have spent a certain amount of computational energy solving a complex mathematical problem. Mining is the biggest culprit in the energy life cycle of Bitcoin. Mining bitcoin, as we briefly touched on, is the technical term for proof of work (PoW). It is what verifies the network and transactions and makes the whole thing work. There are people in the community with giant mining operations, and that uses the biggest share of energy. I have been one of those people, so I guess I am implicated, too.

The environmental impact of Bitcoin did not come to the forefront of public consciousness until Elon Musk decided to tweet about Bitcoin's energy consumption. Musk tends to flip-flop in his opinions of crypto. And being a billionaire, he seems to enjoy the impact of his words—judging from his statements on the market and his own company's stock—and he has a history of jumping on bandwagons. One day he says he loves Bitcoin, the next day he's on board with Dogecoin, then a few months later he is back on the Bitcoin train again. And he moves markets—people will buy and sell based on his opinion.

Despite whatever criticisms or praise he might be due, he raised a valid concern: Is Bitcoin bad for the environment? The answer to that question has a huge impact on Bitcoin's life expectancy. If Bitcoin is not sustainable in terms of energy and material consumption, how will it survive in the face of increasing pressures to combat climate change through any and all means necessary?

We can't deny that Bitcoin uses more energy annually than many small countries. As of this writing, Bitcoin uses approximately 97.6 terawatt hours (TWh) per year, which is more than, say, the 82 TWh used by the entire country of Belgium or 74.9 TWh used in Chile, according to the Cambridge Centre for Alternative Finance (CCAF).[1] It's staggering. (Although it is a drop in the ocean compared to China's 6,453 TWh or the US's 3,843 TWh.) There is also a lot of electronic waste from discarded hardware used for mining. At the same time, the modern-day banking system, or even the gold industry, uses much more energy and electricity—significantly more than crypto. Not to mention that there are just one hundred corporations that are responsible for a whopping 71 percent of greenhouse gas emissions,[2] so there are much bigger offenders out there.

You could argue in that sense that Bitcoin is *more* efficient than most real currencies. It is certainly more efficient than the dollar. I mean, think of all the paper produced and used just for fiat. In this day and age, it is surprising we even use paper and coins as currency. That,

---

[1] US Energy Information Administration, "Country Data," 2019 estimates (or most recent available year), Cambridge Bitcoin Electricity Consumption Index.

[2] Dr. Paul Griffin, *CDP Carbon Majors Report 2017* (London: Carbon Majors Database, 2017).

too, is an energy drain. Take the penny—it costs more to make and distribute a penny than what it's worth, and its production involves environmentally harmful mining of finite materials like zinc and copper. And while many federal mints have made concerted efforts to improve sustainability, they still demand huge water, electricity, and material resources. Not to mention they still utilize carcinogenic chemicals in the process. The fiat system produces a lot of waste, whereas Bitcoin is elegantly simple.

And do other energy-consuming industries or fiat currencies benefit the public at large? Does their impact justify their energy usage?

A lot of energy that Bitcoin uses is cast-off energy, energy that is going to waste anyway. For example, you will often find giant mining farms near hydropower plants or wind farms, which offer cheap rates on "stranded energy," electricity that will not be used locally, is in excess of what can be stored, and would not be profitable to transport. These operations do not rely on coal power or other dirty energy. It is actually in miners' interests not to use energy from fossil fuels, if for no other reason than the fact that fossil fuel prices are steadily rising globally. A lot of miners have moved to Canada or places in the US where there is a lot of cheap, excess energy.

> **The fiat system produces a lot of waste, whereas Bitcoin is elegantly simple.**

This means that Bitcoin also uses a lot of renewable energy. Different studies indicate that between 39 percent[3] and 73 percent[4] of Bitcoin's

---

3   Blandin et al., *3rd Global Cryptoasset Benchmarking Study* (Cambridge Centre for Alternative Finance Publications, 2020).

4   Christopher Bendiksen and Samuel Gibbons, *The Bitcoin Mining Network: Trends, Average Creation Costs, Electricity Consumption & Sources* (CoinShares Research, 2019).

energy use is carbon neutral. It might seem like a wide range, but even the lower end is higher than most of the US grid. And once bitcoin is mined, the energy required to process transactions is pretty negligible. There is a strong argument to be made that eventually mining could be entirely carbon neutral.

Some proponents even see the potential of Bitcoin as a new funding source for renewable energy in places where government subsidies aren't available and private corporations have lost interest because of low returns. Crypto mining could both provide the start-up funds for construction of new renewable energy sites and become the primary customers. Meanwhile, the clean energy supply makes its way out to the rest of the community.

Arguably, these kinds of metrics don't reveal the full picture. As we discussed in the previous chapter, there is nothing else like Bitcoin or crypto. It is a totally new, revolutionary invention in terms of money, finance, and technology. So these kinds of comparisons are incomplete at best and deeply flawed at worst.

To my mind, the energy use is going toward a good cause when compared to energy consumed by the banking system, which is crippling our society and inflating our money away. In my view, it comes down to perspective. And though I look up to Musk—undeniably, he has done some incredible things—he is not an authority on all subjects. And his opinions are not gospel. I do not think that the energy question or environmental impact will be the downfall of Bitcoin. I think there are a lot of viable solutions and improvements to be made on the industry's energy use, sure, but I also think that the crypto project is worth the energy it does consume.

Is Mining for You?

So that leads us to our next question. Is bitcoin mining still a profitable endeavor? And what do you need to do it? As we'll see, these questions in some ways are directly tied to the discussion of energy and environment.

I ran a large mining facility in Oregon for a couple years. When I got into the crypto space, I was intrigued by mining. I knew that with a great enough initial investment you could make a lot of money, if you did it at scale. I started doing it with computer graphics cards used for gaming. So I built the miners from scratch. I had to buy and assemble the various parts. And machines used for mining back then were less energy intensive.

Now ASICs are plug and play miners that basically start doing the work right away. People think if they just buy one ASIC miner for a couple thousand, they will make money, but in reality they will make very little. The market fluctuates in a way that changes how much you earn. Takeaway pay varies over time; it is not fixed. The longer you can hold on to the bitcoin you earn, the longer it has to appreciate, and the greater value gained. It seems straightforward enough, but you need to dedicate a portion of your earnings to business expenses. It becomes a massive headache if you don't know what you are doing. Sometimes people end up in the hole and earning less than their electricity costs and related expenditures. And you have to remember that you are in competition with big mining farms that usually have hundreds of machines and access to cheap energy.

I generally advise people new to the space not to get into mining unless they are serious and have the knowledge, start-up capital, and equipment. Realistically you need hundreds or thousands of miners. It is a lot more work than people think. It is not really something you do as a hobby. Besides massive energy consumption, there are technical and logistical complications. You need knowledge of HVAC systems and airflow, since the equipment produces a large volume of hot air—the space can get up to 120 degrees Fahrenheit. Circuits and wires can melt in that kind of heat. You need proper ventilation, which is tricky in a large space. On top of that, you need good Wi-Fi. You have to have an ethernet connection that does not go down, since you need it to be running 24-7. Every minute that a miner is not running, you are essentially losing money. There is also routine maintenance required. Miners need to be replaced every couple of years for more competitive or energy efficient models. A hash rate is a unit of work for a computer, like an acre is a unit of land. There is a hash network for Bitcoin and other proof of work blockchains—which we'll get into—that increases as more people want to mine. So when it goes up, your miners make less because it is more competitive, and vice versa. So if you were to think of a hash network as an acre of farmable land, the more people harvesting from it, the less each person takes away because each acre has a limit to its yield capacity.

In other words, changes in the network and the macro Bitcoin economy impact mining profitability. There are a lot of variables and a lot of unknowns. For example, China had long been a hot spot for bitcoin mining because of cheap energy costs and generally low cost of living and doing business. Many miners tapped into the cheap hydropower available there, particularly in Sichuan, Yunnan, and Xinjiang, but many more were relying on coal, which China utilizes heavily. Prior to energy consumption crackdowns and hard caps on carbon emissions, more than half of China's energy was from coal—that is a lot of dirty energy in a country with a population of 1.5 billion. So when China banned bitcoin miners in May 2021—primarily in an effort to meet its 2030 carbon neutrality goals—those miners went offline or were forced to move their operations to different countries in what some people call the great mining migration. As a result, the Bitcoin hash rate went down dramatically, meaning there was less competition.

Best of Both Worlds

Some places, like Texas, are miner-friendly and are actively trying to attract miners. The state boasts an abundance of clean, renewable energy and legal protections for bitcoin miners. Texas became the second US state to pass legislation that explicitly recognizes Bitcoin and cryptocurrency in commercial law. And as far as energy costs, Texas has a deregulated power grid with a wide range of suppliers to choose from. It is a global leader in wind energy. Another perk—bitcoin miners can actually sell excess energy back to the grid.

So the energy problem does not necessarily originate with Bitcoin. A lot depends on where the energy is coming from, and much of that depends on a state or country's energy policies. Today, hydropower, wind, tidal, nuclear, and other forms of clean energy are revolutionizing energy usage. These offer a solution to Bitcoin's energy controversy.

Ultimately, it comes down to whether you think Bitcoin justifies its energy use. Other industries use even more, and what are they contributing back? It might be better to turn our attention to countries and corporations producing dirty energy when they could be transitioning to clean energy alternatives. I think a lot of the negative coverage comes from crypto-critics who are using the energy question as a weapon to malign Bitcoin as a whole to advance their own agendas and interests.

Proof of Work versus Proof of Stake

But there are also other options, alternatives to energy-intensive proof of work cryptos like Bitcoin, options that mean you do not have to run giant mining warehouses that consume huge amounts of electricity. There is proof of history, proof of concept, proof of spacetime—most of them are pretty obscure and mostly irrelevant, but theoretically, if you can create a blockchain people can contribute to and create a consensus method for it, then you can use it.

One of the most popular, successful alternatives is called proof of stake (PoS). The main difference between proof of stake and proof of work is how the network creates consensus on the blockchain. In proof of stake, instead of dedicating computer power to the network to validate transactions, a "stake" of crypto assets is delegated to the network. That small stake gives you a "digital vote" into the network for signing transactions.

It sounds complicated, but let's have a look at an example to break it down. Take Cardano, a public blockchain platform that uses proof of stake. Say you have $100,000. You can stake it, meaning you delegate that money to the Cardano network by putting it in a secure wallet that you control, and you freeze that money for a period of time. For as long as it sits frozen in that wallet, you have a vote to sign transactions on that block in the blockchain. Your likelihood to sign a transaction is dictated by the percentage you have delegated. Another way to think of it is like a fixed deposit that pays a specific interest rate at the end of a fixed period of time. When you delegate your stake to the network, just like mining earns you rewards in exchange for your computing power, you earn a dividend as long as your assets are staked to the network. Essentially it is a vote of confidence in the network.

Some tokens have higher yields, some have lower—anything from 1 to 2 percent to 12 to 14 percent based on the particular conventions of the cryptocurrency. So staking is an attractive form of investment, especially for so-called whales (people who have very hefty crypto holdings). A 1 percent yield of $1 million in crypto equates to 10,000 free dollars per year. Better yet, a 10 percent yield means $100,000 at the end of the year, virtually risk-free, just for staking your assets. It is easy passive income.

But this method is open to the criticism that proof of stake benefits the wealthy—the whales—over the smaller holders—the shrimps. A wealthy person has the opportunity to make much more money. I don't really share that critique. We can all make money from it. And proof of stake is not intended to redistribute wealth or earnings or anything. It is simply a method for strengthening the network by offering rewards in exchange for participation.

As it relates to the question of environmental sustainability, proof of stake obviates the need for all the equipment, electricity, and logistics necessary in proof of work platforms. It requires less computing power and therefore less energy. More importantly, it has proven to work well. It is risk averse and safe. And it's popular. Ethereum is slowly converting from proof of work to proof of stake—very slowly, but they are getting there.

Meanwhile, it incentivizes people to keep their money on the network rather than buying, selling, and moving it. It helps take some of the volatility out of the equation.

Bitcoin will probably never adapt proof of stake, even though other projects are likely to switch to it in the future. Bitcoin has such a big network that it is very difficult for people to come to consensus on how to update and change it. You need agreement among a huge number of different actors. On the other hand, knowing Bitcoin is resistant to change is an asset: it gives people confidence in its durability.

Bitcoin is in many ways simpler than other cryptos. Projects like Ethereum, for example, need more flexibility because there is so much utility to them, so many functions and actors using the technology. In contrast, Bitcoin's simplicity is part of its appeal. I'm on the side of those who say, "I hope Bitcoin never changes." I think it is essentially fine the way it is, even if proof of work isn't ideal.

There is a finite amount of bitcoin: twenty-one million. After that, no more will be created or destroyed. Lost bitcoin is out of circulation but not technically destroyed. At some point in time, the bitcoin supply will be fully mined. To slow down the rate of inflation, every four years, the rate of money rewarded for mining is cut in half—the block reward is halved on a regular schedule. The current block reward rate is 6.25 bitcoins. So in the long term, it is a deflationary asset. It also means that the profit margins on mining bitcoin diminish over time. After the mining ceases—in the year 2140—all bitcoin will be in circulation. It has a model that won't change.

> **Bitcoin's simplicity is part of its appeal.**

Each crypto project has its own tokenomics, which we'll review later. That just refers to each token's monetary rules that ensure it remains sustainable. In Bitcoin's case, it is thought that Satoshi was fed up with the financial system's collapse, the predatory banking and lending system, and inflationary monetary policy; hence the creation of a decentralized, secure, mostly stable asset like Bitcoin. Just look at examples like Venezuela, where people are investing in Bitcoin to circumvent the country's corruption and inflation. Or the recent adoption of Bitcoin as legal currency in El Salvador.

You want price to be dictated by demand and use rather than by some entity pumping more bitcoin into the network, as is the case with central banks and fiat currency. Trillions of dollars are printed, and often just to lend to other economies, inflating the global money supply and eroding the purchasing power of the dollars in your pocket (and keeping interest rates down). And all kinds of concomitant problems ranging from debt to dirty money in the system and banks loaning out our money on a fractional reserve system. The economics of real currency are vastly different from the tokenomics of Bitcoin.

Which brings us to our next discussion. As we've touched on, there are alternatives to Bitcoin (although Bitcoin's market value still overshadows all its competitors). What are some of the other major tokens? How do they differ from Bitcoin? And how will their success or failure affect Bitcoin and the landscape of cryptocurrency in the future?

CHAPTER 5
A CRYPTO-COPIA

We've taken a good look at Bitcoin, but there is a lot more to crypto and blockchain than Bitcoin. So what else is out there? I have mentioned a few other altcoins, and we have even gotten glimpses of how they differ from Bitcoin. Now we are going to examine the world beyond Bitcoin more closely. I have chosen ten other tokens that are important to understand as alternatives to Bitcoin.

Bitcoin is more a currency than it is anything else. Some tokens have followed that model, but the most successful ones have gone a different way in applying blockchain technology to real-world problems.

Ethereum (ETH)

We can't talk about altcoins without talking about Ethereum. It is the number two crypto by market capitalization (or market cap), meaning the total dollar market value of the company's shares of stock. In spring 2021, its market cap hit over $482 billion, and ether, the native currency

> **Bitcoin is more a currency than it is anything else.**

of Ethereum, peaked at over $4,000 per token. And it is the first blockchain in the space to even mention smart contracts, let alone employ them with such efficiency. Pretty much every innovation that has happened in blockchain has happened in Ethereum. It's got a lot of momentum. There is a reason why it's the second biggest in the world, a spot that it has a firm grip on, right below Bitcoin—despite the perennial rumors of so-called Ethereum killers.

Like Bitcoin, Ethereum lets you use digital money without having to go through third parties like banks or payment providers. So you can send and receive ether just like bitcoin. Ethereum also uses a proof of work system, like Bitcoin. But overall, Ethereum is more of a utility or a decentralized operating system than a currency. So it has a ton of unrealized value (along with much realized value as well).

It is such a useful network that a lot of the other tokens and projects are Ethereum-based—in fact, there are nearly three thousand decentralized apps (also called dapps) running on the Ethereum blockchain. These range from lending services, smart contracts, gaming and in-game purchases—and with thousands of projects, you can imagine there is a lot of variety.

Cardano (ADA)

Cardano was first released in 2017. Its founder, Charles Hoskinson, was one of the creators of Ethereum, and he left to form his company, Input Output Hong Kong (IOHK). Cardano is his alternative to Ethereum, a vision that addresses Ethereum's shortcomings, such as scalability and energy efficiency. It is popular at the moment and will be for the foreseeable future. As of this writing, it is one of the top five biggest blockchains by market cap at $76.6 billion—despite ADA's token price hovering between two and three dollars.

The entryway into Cardano is much easier than it is with Ethereum. To work with Ethereum as a developer, you have to learn Solidity, which is the Ethereum coding language. That is like saying you have to learn Norwegian to order a hamburger at McDonald's in the US when you already speak English. It is just not practical. Cardano, on the other hand, uses Haskell, which is a general-purpose coding language with a lot of flexibility, which makes it more attractive to developers.

Cardano is also one of the first blockchains to utilize proof of stake and show that it works. They already have a number of use cases for things like credential verification for academic certifications, anticounterfeiting for retail goods, and supply chain tracking in agriculture. Basically, what Ethereum is trying to establish with Ethereum 2.0, Cardano nailed right out of the gate. This, too, is why it has appreciated in value a great deal.

Presently, Cardano can pretty much do everything Ethereum can. I have been telling people for the last three years they should consider investing in or building on it. And that was when it cost two cents apiece! But it is not about the money. Cardano is proof positive that you do not need to rely on Ethereum to lead the way in crypto. Cardano has really opened up the space to developers to try alternative blockchains to Ethereum.

Solana (SOL)

Solana is another token that is also getting a lot of attention. Even though it was initially released in April 2019, the buzz around it burst on the scene, seemingly out of nowhere, in spring 2021. They have marketed themselves well as the fastest, cheapest blockchain out there. They claim to support fifty thousand transactions per second. It is without a doubt a blockchain that is built for developers; it is incredibly easy to build on. That is their brand. And they have followed through on their promises thus far.

Founder Anatoly Yakovenko's whole aim was to develop a decentralized network that matched the performance of a single node. So when we talked about the Byzantine Generals Problem, Yakovenko was basically looking to build a network of generals that operated so fluidly and cooperatively that it functioned the same way a single general giving orders would. Like Cardano, it is a proof of stake system, but it has incorporated a number of other technological innovations to achieve that level of performance.

Consequently, Solana has garnered a lot of projects, some of which we have featured on my podcast.

A lot of my guests were talking about Solana, and I was like, "What the hell is this thing?" And then by summer 2021, it exploded in growth. It is growing quickly across various niches like DeFi, NFTs, and Web 3.0 developers. It is kind of the new, hip blockchain. I believe it could even surpass Cardano or Ethereum in the future. Of course, it is a young project, and such projects tend to experience setbacks as they grow and mature. So there will be challenges in the future. But it has definitely emerged red-hot onto the market and shows a lot of promise.

So these three blockchains—Ethereum, Cardano, and Solana—focus a lot on smart contracts and what you can do in terms of building an app. They fulfill similar functions: launching tokens, creating apps for games, creating NFTs, and so on. Other blockchains are more niche but still important for understanding the whole scope of blockchain, as we will discuss next.

Filecoin (FIL)

Made by Protocol Labs, Filecoin's launch was atypical. There was no initial coin offering (ICO, or the cryptocurrency parallel of an IPO); instead, they started with a simple agreement for future tokens, or SAFT agreement. What this means is that an investor offers to buy shares in a company but at a future date, at a set price. It is a kind of security for the eventual transfer of digital tokens: It is a way to help cryptocurrency ventures fundraise without violating any laws, and it gives investors an added level of protection. Just like an ICO is the crypto version of an IPO, SAFT agreements are the crypto version of simple agreements for future equity, or SAFE agreements for real currency investments.

Filecoin launched their SAFT on a platform called CoinList. When I first invested at around five dollars a token, it guaranteed me a certain amount of filecoin at that price when the project finally launched. This approach let them secure a number of backers in advance.

What makes Filecoin unique is that as a blockchain, it focuses on *decentralized storage,* which is important to Web 3.0 because decentralized functions don't rely on a single point of failure. Decentralized storage is displacing apps like Google Drive, Dropbox, or Microsoft OneDrive, which are expensive and raise concerns about privacy, security, and confidentiality (despite the promises these companies make). Decentralized storage is not on most people's radar yet, but it is going to be pivotal in creating a new internet and its abundance of data.

Filecoin is not the first to solve this problem, but it is the first to do it well.

I have had Jonathan Victor, the product manager of Protocol Labs, on the podcast to discuss Filecoin and its InterPlanetary File System (IPFS).

It is becoming more popular to make money through the Filecoin network than it is to mine cryptocurrency. As we discussed, mining is an expensive proposition. If you want to stake it, you need to have a lot of it to earn decent dividends. But with Filecoin, it is simple and a fairly decent way to earn passive income. It is similar to proof of work systems like Bitcoin except you are *lending* unused storage space on your hard drive or computer to the network. In exchange, you get compensated in filecoin based on what you contribute. And, also like Bitcoin, the supply is limited; the filecoin supply is set to be capped at two billion, 70 percent of which will go to miners.

Many Chinese miners who were shut down by the government moved to decentralized storage and to Filecoin in particular as a way to make money. Because it is so new, there is less competition than in mining bitcoin, which means there is a lower barrier to entry onto the network. (If it seems like China comes up a lot in this book, it's because it is such an important player in the space, and what happens there can have a lot of influence on the crypto market as a whole.)

Civic (CVC)

Civic was founded by Vinny Lingham, whom I have hosted on the *BlockHash* podcast. Vinny is an entrepreneur from South Africa. (He might be familiar to some readers as one of the sharks from *Shark Tank South Africa*.) He is eager to help people protect their identity through blockchain. He is a vocal presence on social media and a cheerleader for various other protocols. And he does a lot of good work in South Africa through his NGO, Silicon Cape, to help build Cape Town into one the next big tech hubs, like Silicon Valley. I greatly value his opinions.

Civic is a smaller blockchain, and as such it does not get as much attention. But I want to highlight it because it is involved in an important and growing niche—verifying your identity anywhere in the world using blockchain.

The COVID-19 pandemic provided a great opportunity for a use case in blockchain. As people began to receive vaccinations, governments grappled with the puzzle of how to verify that information for things like international travel, employment, or attending large events and gatherings. Being able to verify that someone has received a vaccine is an example of how blockchain can be used. And Civic has helped make that possible. Civic is pioneering the concept of global identity verification across industries. They are helping companies meet know your customers (KYC) and anti-money laundering (AML) requirements, taking away the burden of the trust factor, and making the whole process seamless.

> **The COVID-19 pandemic provided a great opportunity for a use case in blockchain.**

It is easy to see the widespread applications this can have for everyday document verification like passports, driver's licenses, residence permits—you name it. And that is going to be all the more important in a digital world increasingly inhabited by bots and scammers.

It may not sound as exciting as DeFi or NFTs, but it has profound implications for how business is done. Overall it will make things more secure, more efficient, and faster. It's an important niche that deserves our attention.

Uniswap (UNI)

Uniswap is more a protocol than a blockchain, as it was built on the Ethereum blockchain (one of the Ethereum-based dapps mentioned earlier). It is well known for kicking off the decentralized finance (DeFi) movement. It does two things. One, it takes power away from centralized financial entities, giving it back to the public. Two, it offers financial tools that are often inaccessible to certain segments of the population.

Uniswap makes financial transactions simple and seamless. It does everything from lending to decentralized credit scores to offering collateralized options, trading with leverage, easily swapping one crypto for another at a low fee, reducing the friction of multiple verification steps, and setting up an account on an exchange. One really unique aspect is its use of the automated market maker (AMM) system. So instead of supply and demand dictating market value, as in Wall Street style trades, AMM lets Uniswap use a pricing algorithm to set the price of assets. This incentivizes investors to provide liquidity and make exchanges at a set market price—essentially reducing some of the volatility of trade.

There are now many players in the DeFi space, but to me Uniswap is the paragon. And they have maintained the biggest market share, despite the competition nipping at their heels.

Hedera Hashgraph (HBAR)

Technically Hedera Hashgraph is not even a blockchain. But I think it is important to show there are alternatives to blockchain itself, including some very good options. Hedera Hashgraph is one of the good ones.

Some devotees of blockchain are resentful of HBAR because it is a threat to blockchain. Opponents view it as too centralized. But in all my years in the space talking to so many creators, Dr. Leemon Baird, Hedera Hashgraph's founder and chief scientist, is one of the smartest people I've ever talked to. He is a prominent ideas man and has a lot to say on the future of the crypto space. Through our conversations and other research, I have come to understand what Hedera Hashgraph does, and I think there are many misconceptions around it that are worth clearing up.

So, first off, what is a hashgraph? Simply put, it is a graph of transactions that works on this idea called gossip protocol. It's similar to blockchain but achieves consensus a different way. Everyone who makes a transaction on a hashgraph is "gossiping" that information to someone else. It creates a vast flow of information that allows everyone to reach consensus on what is happening. If blockchain is a Legoland of transactions competitively mined to create consensus, hashgraph is a group of ladies at lunch who all decide that Karen is definitely sleeping with her son's teacher, and that word becomes gospel. That is the brief, nontechnical summary. So it functions like blockchain but uses a different scheme.

What makes Hadera Hashgraph so interesting is that it is significantly faster than most blockchains, is very easy to build on, and has already secured some of the biggest partnerships in the world (with Google, IBM, Deutsche Telekom, and Boeing, for instance). Even the Federal Reserve has looked at their technology for launching a coin (CBDCs are a topic we'll discuss later.) It is a decentralized protocol, but there is a patent on the hashgraph, so technically no one else can create a project using hashgraph (blockchain, in contrast, is public domain). This sets it apart, and many people in the space like it for that reason because it is centralized and controlled. (Others dislike it for the same reason.)

There are valid critiques to be made—without doubt—but simply being "controlled" does not mean it's bad. It is a very effective tool. There is a time and place for using centralized things. And I think HBAR might be the one to prove it.

So those are what I would call the major players and a good mix of the different applications and manifestations of blockchain and crypto. It is a small sample of the massive variety of tokens that are out there—with more on the way still in development. It is easy to reduce the crypto space to Bitcoin, which mainstream media tends to do. But there is so much more to it. The really exciting stuff is still on the horizon.

There are a handful of other notable cryptos that are worth mentioning briefly. I won't go into as much detail here, but each of these three has its place in the history and future of the space.

Ripple (XRP)

As of this writing, Ripple is dogged by lawsuits and an SEC investigation. The SEC wants to classify ripple tokens as a security rather than as a currency. This is going to be a really critical case because many other blockchains have similar concerns. The SEC decision will have major implications for the whole industry. So now all eyes are on the legal tussle between the SEC and Ripple, which insists its token is a currency, as it has always stated.

If Ripple loses to the SEC, many other blockchains could be legally reclassified as securities or property.

The XRP token itself is very fast and convenient for making remittances. Ripple can clear cross-border remittances in around two seconds. Many banks have adopted its technology. The federal government has also looked into using Ripple's platform to replace the SWIFT bank wire system. So there is clearly a lot of potential value there. And if Ripple comes out the other side of this, it could steal some of Bitcoin's market share, as Bitcoin is used heavily for moving money quickly over borders.

Stablecoins

With stablecoins, the value is pegged to fiat currency like the dollar. This makes it easier to trade back and forth between fiat and crypto, makes markets more liquid, and gives people more incentive to buy and sell. The idea is that having a cryptocurrency tied to a real reserve asset might lend it more stability and help crypto-skeptics get on board. Proponents see it as a best of both worlds solution, but viewed from a different angle, it's a half measure that keeps power vested in traditional financial institutions.

Dogecoin (DOGE)

Dogecoin gets a lot of press; it has become a cultural touchstone. Elon Musk is a frequent, high-profile commentor on Dogecoin. Created as a joke (based on the popular Shiba Inu meme), it is now taken seriously as a currency. I won't invest in it personally because it is too unpredictable, but it is a good, solid, reliable blockchain—technically speaking. It is fast and convenient to use. More and more retailers are accepting DOGE. It has a growing infrastructure and a big pop culture presence, especially among younger users.

I doubt Dogecoin will ever surpass Bitcoin or replace it, but it could prove to be prolific as a currency that people use commercially.

Even with all the variety of tokens out there, I don't think any will ever displace Bitcoin as the frontrunner in the market. Bitcoin and Satoshi have created the perfect, decentralized money. So many people now own it, and its tokenomics model is so advanced, it would be hard for any other project to catch up. And after only one decade, its market cap is gargantuan: It is crazy that one single protocol could be worth a trillion dollars in value. Who knows? In a couple more decades, it could reach $20 or $30 trillion—more valuable globally than gold.

It will remain *the* currency of the internet. "If you come for the king, you best not miss." And I can't see any other crypto making that shot.

But as I have said elsewhere in this book and on my podcast, crypto and blockchain are about more than market share and making bank. The really cool thing about altcoins is their potential to reshape the way we do basically everything, to revolutionize the entire digital landscape. So seeing those projects develop and come to fruition is still what excites me.

Next up, we'll have a look at another aspect of the market that's starting to emerge. So far, we've focused on non-fungible, decentralized tokens. But as you'll see, there is a whole lot more to the universe of cryptocurrencies than you can imagine.

CHAPTER 6
NIFTY NFTS

What do a pixelated cartoon of Serena Williams, a little girl giving serious side-eye, and a cartoon ape wearing a safari hat have in common? Believe it or not, they are all examples of non-fungible tokens, or NFTs.

What does that mean? Well, there are two types of crypto, generally speaking. The type we see all the time—and that we have been discussing up to this point—are cryptocurrencies that are fungible and can be exchanged for other tokens of that same kind. If I have a bitcoin and you have a bitcoin, we could swap them and still have one bitcoin each. If you gave me one dollar, and I gave you one, we'd each have a buck.

NFTs, in contrast, are the opposite. They are not fungible, meaning each one is unique. You cannot create two NFTs that are the same. You can create an image and use it to create an NFT over and over, but each token in the codebase or smart contract is original. When you create an NFT through a smart contract, that contract will mint the token onto its respective blockchain. So, for example, say you are using the Ethereum blockchain to create an NFT. When you mint that specific NFT, a record goes on the blockchain, and numerically that block is unique. So the image may not be unique, but the block on the blockchain is, and that's what imparts value to the NFT.

OpenSea is the biggest NFT marketplace. I spoke with Devin Finzer, the cofounder and CEO, on *BlockHash* when OpenSea was in its infancy and virtually unknown even in the crypto world. Admittedly, it would be harder to get him on the podcast today if I didn't already know him, since now he is one of the major players in the space. Before founding OpenSea, he worked at Google and Pinterest on their growth teams. He's a young guy, really smart, really ambitious, and looks a little like Ryan Reynolds.

The big goal of his project is to leverage Ethereum's open protocols to enable users to buy and sell any Ethereum-based asset. It also now uses other blockchains, including Polygon, Tezos, and probably Solana and others in the near future. Devin and his cofounder, Alex Atallah, have done an incredible job creating the biggest NFT marketplace in the world, and one that is open to everyone. It is simple to use and free if you are a creator. There are no membership or sign-up fees. You do not even have to spend money to create your own NFT. You only spend money if you sell one. They are genuinely interested in making a space for creating, curating, and collecting art and supporting artists. And that was something of a paradigm shift away from the Bitcoin model—where investors are mostly interested in buying and flipping for profit.

NFTs emerged not that long ago. The first proto-NFT was minted in 2014, but it was a one-off, a demonstration that this kind of thing was possible with blockchain. Then, in 2015, Ethereum introduced its first NFT project: Etheria. The 457 NFTs from that went largely unsold until 2021, believe it or not. Each one was hardcoded to one ether token. So if you had bought in back then, it would have been worth only 43 cents. They ended up selling for over $1.4 million.

But really it was not until 2017, right around the time Ethereum's blockchain went live, that NFTs started gaining traction. Some of the first were CryptoKitties and CryptoPunks. Thousands of them were given out for free, which is crazy when you see how much they are worth now. They were the first use cases and have since become highly coveted digital collectibles, genuine art pieces.

Most NFTs are Ethereum-based (using the ERC-721 standard), but others use Solana (which we talked about in the last chapter), FLOW, and Tezos (more altcoins!).

CryptoPunks are hugely popular today; some sell for millions of dollars. Insane numbers. Eye-watering actually. They are 24x24-pixel images, usually of a figure's head and neck. There is nothing particularly special or valuable about them, certainly nothing physically distinct about them, and artistically, they're very simple. Yet they have managed to become *the* big-ticket item, ever since the 2021 NFT boom. Owning one could literally make you a millionaire overnight.

NFTs are a curious thing. No one can really explain why they became so popular so fast. Celebrities touted them, people caught on, interest exploded, and they became a trend. Like a lot of viral trends, NFTs, which are objectively ordinary looking, became subjectively special. It's the same kind of viral sensation you see elsewhere in the digital world. Something catches fire and spreads, without any real rhyme or reason.

That's not to diminish the value of NFTs or their place in the crypto space. They have a bright future and solve tons of real-world problems, despite the surface-level fad.

I think a major contributing factor to the popularity of NFTs

> **NFTs are a curious thing. No one can really explain why they became so popular so fast.**

was when Christie's began to list them. Many artists had previously listed their NFTs to create provenance with their work and be able to sell their art digitally, earning royalties on secondary sales and so forth. So they have been a fringe part of the art world for a couple of years. But Christie's adoption brought them into the mainstream and validated them. When Mike Winkelmann's (a.k.a. Beeple's) piece *The First 5,000 Days*, a digital collage, sold for $69 million, it was the first blockchain-based item sold by a major auction house (making Beeple the third most expensive living artist at auction).

With that move, Christie's single-handedly legitimized NFTs as art. Now people are frantically looking for the next big thing—buying, selling, investing, speculating, and trading NFTs. Musicians, celebrities, and others are creating their own collections or utilizing NFTs one way or another.

Why Are They Important?

NFTs solve critical problems for individuals and businesses. Specifically, look at the art world. Painters, drawers, sketchers, sculptors, artists of all sorts can use NFTs to prove provenance: proof of who the artist is, when a work was created, if it's an original or a replica. Obviously that is hugely important to the art world. Plus it tracks the chain of custody—who owns it—and determines who should receive royalties. There is a lot of purported Renaissance art whose provenance cannot be proved. There are works that even experts have difficulty determining whether they are authentic, forgeries, or perhaps painted by someone else in the artist's studio but not the artist himself.

So, for artists, proving provenance is integral to preserving the integrity of their art. It also gives them a direct line of communication to potential buyers. They don't need to convince a gallery or curator.

It is encouraging new artists to venture into the digital art world as a new and exciting medium. And I suspect it will revolutionize the whole art world.

Musicians, too, can benefit from the technology. The music industry is full of nightmare stories of musicians who sign onto a bad contract and then lose the intellectual property rights to their own work, or they get locked into a contract and can't take their music elsewhere, or they get screwed over on royalties they are owed or deserve. Taylor Swift famously got "trapped" by a record label when she was young and her popularity was just starting to grow. But one company owns most of her work, and now she's boxed in.

Record companies have been taking advantage of musicians for decades. NFTs help empower artists to take control of their intellectual property and the things that go with it. They can drop a new song and attach it to an NFT or collect royalties on their work when their music is used by a third party—all without a record label or middlemen. Some smart contracts have even been encoded to add royalties on resale, so the artist can still benefit as their work accrues value. No more van Goghs starving in their attic apartments.

Athletes are also getting in the game. They are using NFTs to market and monetize their name, image, and likeness so that they can make money beyond the sports conglomerates and corporate sponsors. College athletes, who are tightly—some might say unfairly—regulated by the NCAA regarding the ways they can make money, are also using it. Only recently, in July 2021, did the NCAA finally allow players to make money off things like endorsements, autograph signing, and personal appearances. In response to the (temporary) rule change, some have started creating their own NFT trading cards.

Tampa Bay tight end Rob Gronkowski did an NFT release where he auctioned off NFT sports cards depicting him in his four championship games. One NFT had unlockable content that offered a meeting with Gronkowski for the lucky winner. (You can attach bonuses to an NFT, meaning something digital or physical comes with the purchase.)

LeBron James sold an NFT of a video clip of himself dunking for $200,000. In fact, the network he used, NBA Top Shot, is one of the most successful NFT platforms out there. It started in 2019 as a collaboration between Dapper Labs, which creates dapps on the FLOW blockchain, and the National Basketball Players Association, the labor union for the NBA. In an era when labor rights have been steadily undermined and eaten away at for decades, it is a really progressive, groundbreaking move.

Basically, NFTs eliminate the middlemen in stagnant, ossified, hierarchical industries. And the sky is the limit. Charities can use it to raise money for their causes. Like so much in the blockchain universe, it empowers the individual and eliminates the need for powerful middlemen to protect or sell your work.

I think it is important to note that without Devin Finzer's contribution to the space—that is, OpenSea—CryptoKitties and CryptoPunks would never be what they are, digital artists would not have the recognition they have, Beeple would not be a household name (in the crypto and art worlds anyway). It is a marvelous platform that benefits artist and patrons alike, free of censorship or top-down control.

The whole NFT industry might have disappeared into irrelevancy, but I believe Devin's stewardship helped lead us to what we have today: a thriving and disruptive industry that is here to stay. He is another young crypto visionary.

How Do I Buy an NFT?

NFTs are getting snatched up by both traditional art buyers who are speculating on NFTs as the next big thing in the art world and younger folk who have made a lot of money in crypto and want to diversify into NFTs to protect their assets. The buyers' market can't be generalized broadly. It's new money, old money, Gen Z, boomers, everyone. It is trendy and popular now, and a lot of people want to get in the game. Even when the trend fades and the market cools, NFTs will always have value, especially the highly sought-after pieces. Just like Picasso will never go out of style, so, too, will CryptoPunks live in infamy.

So how do you go about buying your own NFT? Let's say you want to buy a CryptoPunk on OpenSea. OpenSea uses a third-party blockchain application, MetaMask, which is like a digital wallet that works in your Chrome browser. It gives you a digital profile and automatically logs you into OpenSea securely. That application keeps it as a pure marketplace and a simple platform.

Then you transfer some Ethereum into your MetaMask wallet, search for your NFT of choice on OpenSea, click "Buy Now," and sign the smart contract by clicking "Sign." OpenSea executes the contract, and boom, you own your first NFT.

If you buy an NFT through an auction, you follow the same process, except of course you must place a bid and cross your fingers—rather than buying it outright.

It's remarkably simple and streamlined.

Other Applications

In addition to being a valuable technology for artists and athletes, there is a landslide of future use cases. These include ticketing, invoicing, and supply chain management. They can be used as a secure way to produce any unique product, whether that is art, identification or legal documents, or branded products. It boosts efficiency in all kinds of markets.

So let's look at how NFTs can work for ticketing. A business or individual can create an NFT that represents a concert or plane ticket, for example. Every seat is a unique block on the blockchain; no two are the same. It is an especially elegant solution for airlines, which often overbook or oversell by selling tickets on multiple sites. Blockchain provides consensus, so it would eliminate this problem. And, as I mentioned, you can attach bonuses to NFTs. So along with your ticket, you might also have bonus videos of places to visit at your destination or a collectible work of art depicting the capital city.

If you buy a ticket as an NFT, you can resell it or give it away easily, creating trade value and boosting the value of the secondary ticket market, which may be advantageous for all parties.

Identification is another use case. If you hold that token, you can verifiably prove that you are you, Brandon is Brandon, Vitalik is Vitalik, Satoshi is—well, no one knows who he is.

Imagine how easy it would be for international travel: Scan a code anywhere in the world, and off you go to your airline gate. But beyond travel, NFTs can be used for almost any kind of identity document or proof of ownership. You could buy a car or a house using NFTs, and because of the high level of security and authentication, as a buyer it would protect you from scams and cut out high-cost middlemen.

You can use NFTs for in-game virtual items in video games. The gaming industry has expanded exponentially and will likely continue to do so—especially as virtual reality, augmented reality, and other technologies continue to grow. The user experience is more customizable, more personal, and more competitive than it used to be. Some e-sports tournaments have more "attendees" than the Super Bowl. With virtual property and virtual goods, the gaming industry has created a whole new marketplace. It opens up a digital realm that is a vast and infinite analog to the real-world economy.

Intellectual property ownership is likely to be another major area of development for NFTs. They can prove that you own a trademark, invented something special, or own certain rights in a contract. IP law can be tricky; it can be extremely onerous to verify who owns what. NFTs are likely to simplify these complications.

The question of provenance that we discussed with artwork can be applied to other industries, too. Knowing when and where something is created, transported, or delivered can be a logistical quagmire in an increasingly complex global supply chain. NFTs enable you to track goods more accurately.

We can use the farm-to-table concept as an example. More consumers are clueing into the hazards of global supply chains and trying to make informed, ethical decisions. If you buy organic steak at the grocery store or order shrimp scampi at a restaurant, how can you be sure of the origin of that food? NFTs let you know how and where it was sourced and follow it along every point in its chain of custody. It is also good for the producer who can make more money by operating more efficiently. If you are that shrimp company, you can learn how much shrimp is actually being consumed and tailor your production to actual consumption. And that benefits the environment, too, by reducing waste and decreasing the likelihood of overfishing. It's a win-win-win.

The retail industry faces similar challenges as consumers move away from fast fashion and opt for more sustainable, ethically produced products.

It adds a lot of value for the end consumer who wants to ensure the provenance and quality of their purchases.

NFTs can be used as an anticounterfeiting measure. They can guarantee an item is authentic. So you can be certain that the Chanel purse or new Yeezy shoes you bought are authentic. Attaching an NFT to such items, which are frequently counterfeited, can provide this assurance. The counterfeit industry is responsible for billions of lost profits each year—not to mention the health risks counterfeit goods pose in the case of cosmetics or consumables. A number of luxury companies are already applying blockchain technology to create NFTs to represent their products to fight against counterfeiting, which has dogged the industry for a long time.

Vouchers, coupons, music, album drops—I am sure in the near future we will see Drake drop an album or the latest single as an NFT. In the next few years, I think we will see some unique ways to sell and auction off NFTs.

The Bottom Line

NFTs prove ownership of *something*. A client and friend of mine, Camilo Restrepo, launched an NFT collection titled *a ToN oF coke*. He came up with the idea of "digital cocaine," but he did it to create a dialogue around the role of cocaine in Colombia's history and shed light on the violence the people of Colombia have endured as a result of this notorious industry. As an artist, he wants to get people to talk and think, especially about controversial subjects. He is trying to call attention to the drug's role in Colombia's frequently dark and troubled history, a recurring motif of his artwork.

He created one thousand NFTs, each one a virtual kilo of cocaine, and sold them on OpenSea. Literally each one is just the image of a white brick, a simple white box. I bought his first one. Within a week they started selling out like crazy. He got a lot of press in Colombian newspapers and in the crypto press.

As an artist, he was struggling to break out, to stand out in a competitive industry, and he saw NFTs as a way of distinguishing himself. And, well, he was right.

Aesthetically, digital art is very subjective as far as whether you think it is good art or not. A lot of it is a throwback to early digital images, so they can be very simple, amateurish even. If I draw a stick figure and some drunk billionaire offers me a million bucks for it, then "the market" values it at a million bucks. Take CryptoPunks: There is nothing special about them per se, but their value is derived from the fact that many people see them as special or desirable. Marx would have a field day with them. Artists understand market dynamics as well as anyone, and they also understand the randomness of the industry. Who makes it big and who toils in obscurity is by and large arbitrary, a matter of chance and circumstance.

Are NFTs a Bubble?

There is a difference between a new asset class and traditional market bubbles. People think if something shoots up radically in value, it makes it a bubble. Obviously the bubble label has been leveled at Bitcoin and crypto. But as a technology, this is not just a fad; it is an original protocol that is solving real-world problems. So NFTs are not just going to disappear.

Sure, the value of certain NFTs have "bubbled up," and their valuation is eventually going to level off. Prices go up and down, as they do in oil, gold, and all kinds of markets. But the notion that NFTs are a bubble that, once it pops, will fade into the ether is misguided.

NFTs have tremendous utility and a bright future, despite whatever price volatility characterizes the market in the years to come.

NFTs are not like other (fungible) tokens or markets where they trade rapidly back and forth. The non-fungibility imparts, to an extent, greater value because they are not quite as liquid. They are not replicable, which helps ensure that they hold their value. And in some sense, they are more reliable, more permanent than traditional art forms. You can spill a glass of wine on the *Mona Lisa*, but you can't spill a glass of wine on a CryptoPunk.

NFTs have tremendous utility and a bright future, despite whatever price volatility characterizes the market in the years to come.

Despite the differences between NFTs and fungible tokens, both adhere to the basic ethos of blockchain we've seen up to this point. They are decentralized, non-fiat currencies. But next up, we'll do a 180 and explore another layer of crypto that encompasses centralized, fiat tokens.

CHAPTER 7
ANOTHER DAY, ANOTHER DOLLAR

CBDC: central bank digital currency. The definition is right there in the name, but to really understand it, you have to consider the question, What is money? And that is a little more abstract.

A digital currency is a currency issued by the governing bank of a country or jurisdiction. In the US, that issuer is the Federal Reserve. In the European Union, it is the European Central Bank. And in the United Kingdom, you have the Bank of England. A CBDC is issued directly through the central bank rather than through the country's treasury.

CBDCs are fairly common now, or at least the idea of them is. Some countries have already adopted them, and many more are considering them. China has what is probably the most popular use case, Digital Currency Electronic Payments (DCEP), issued by the People's Bank of China. The aim is essentially to create a digital currency that can compete with the US dollar globally. China is projected to overtake the US as the biggest economy, and the introduction of DCEP is part of their strategy. And as a communist country, they seek more capital control and surveillance, including of their citizens' use of money and currency.

And so far, they have been fairly successful. They were able to program and introduce it quickly and are already implementing it among their citizens—exchanging analog yuan for digital yuan (yuan being the denomination of China's currency, which is renminbi, or RMB; in other words, yuan: dollar, RMB: USD). But the big news here is that China was the first major country in the world to do this.

As I mentioned, a number of other countries are looking to CBDCs as a way to bring their currencies into the digital age. Sweden has been seeking to create an e-Krona since 2017. The use of cash—specifically point-of-sale cash transactions—in Sweden has dropped substantially. It can be difficult to quantify, but the trend is clear. For example, in a 2010 survey by Sveriges Riksbank, the central bank of Sweden, 39 percent of respondents had used cash for their most recent transaction; by 2020, that figure was down to 9 percent.[5] The same study found that the number of people who had used cash at all in the previous month dropped from 61 percent in 2010 to 50 percent in 2020. A less dramatic drop but significant nonetheless.

The decline is actually a global trend. People are spending more money using credit or debit cards and paying through their phone and online, which increases the utility of a CBDC.

The EU has been exploring the potential of a digital euro and is studying how to develop the infrastructure for it. Singapore's monetary authorities are doing the same. The Bank of Korea in South Korea is running a ten-month pilot program using CBDC. The Bank of Japan has launched a one-year pilot. The UK, Canada, on and on—the move to a digital monetary system through CBDC is a prevalent topic among G20 nations.

---

5   Sveriges Riksbank, "The Use of Cash Is Declining," October 29, 2020, https://www.riksbank.se/the-use-of-cash-is-declining.

CBDCs and the Federal Reserve

Most of the world still looks to the US as a global leader, especially in finance and business, and the US dollar remains the world's reserve currency. So what the US and the Federal Reserve do regarding CBDCs holds a lot of weight. And the world is watching to see if they will unroll a digital dollar, or so-called Fedcoin.

The Fed has been studying it for a long time, and several bills on the subject have been introduced and debated in Congress. The most recent iteration is the Digital Asset Market Structure and Investor Protection Act, H.R. 4741, which was introduced in July 2021. I wish they could give it a shorter name! But in any event, if passed, it will redefine the term "legal tender" in order to give authority to the Federal Reserve to issue its own CBDC. In part, the US has to make *some* move to keep up with China financially and technologically.

> **The move to a digital monetary system through CBDC is a prevalent topic among G20 nations.**

I also believe they are doing it for other reasons, some of which are problematic. Governments may want to move to a CBDC system because it grants them greater surveillance power over transactions: What are you doing with your money? From whom are you receiving it and to whom are you paying it? Are you funding illicit activities? It is a blow to individual freedom to give authorities more snooping powers over what you do with your money. Privacy—financial, digital—is a huge constitutional issue.

One of my guests on *BlockHash*, Danielle DiMartino Booth, has a ton of insight into this question. Danielle has had a distinguished career on both Wall Street and at the Federal Reserve. She was formerly a business columnist at the *Dallas Morning News*, largely writing about her observations on the US economy and financial markets. She also spent nine years at the Federal Reserve Bank of Dallas. She is currently the CEO of Quill Intelligence, providing objective analysis on the financial workings of government and financial institutions at a macro scale. I spoke to her while she was promoting her new book, *Fed Up*, which explains her position on how the Federal Reserve is bad for America.

It is kind of her mission to expose the abuse of power and tunnel vision that the Fed has when it comes to the US economy and the hazards that their policies pose to everyday people. Her point is basically that the Fed is run by a bunch of academics who are ill-equipped to make decisions that affect the real world in such an immediate, material way. They often can't see beyond their "ideal world" economic models. And, ultimately, they are less like James Bond villains and more like Dr. Evil from *Austin Powers*—laughably but dangerously misguided.

Economic control and social coercion are, in my view, also motives for the Fed to develop a CBDC. Simply put, the digital dollar would give the government and the Fed broad control over monetary policy and therefore more control over your daily life. This is the same institution, as DiMartino Booth points out, that created the market conditions that directly led to the housing bubble and recession of 2008.

From there it is a slippery slope for the US to move in the same direction as China with social credit scores. If you're not familiar with the practice—or if you haven't seen the *Black Mirror* episode modeled on it—the Chinese scheme basically uses things like your salary and how you spend it to determine how "good" or "trustworthy" a citizen you are. And that score affects real-life things like your ability to travel or get treated at a hospital, to hold certain jobs, or to take on loans. China should be a cautionary tale for us.

And if history is any indication, the Federal Reserve does not always make the best decisions on how to handle debt obligations, how to respond to economic crises, what kind of monetary policy (inflationary vs. deflationary, etc.) to establish, and so forth. So, personally, I am wary of a Fed-run CBDC.

How Might a Digital Dollar Be Created?

So what happens if the Fed goes through with developing a CBDC? There's a lot of speculation around this question. As of yet, little action has been taken. To build a CBDC, they would need to use blockchain or something similar. This would ensure its functionality and prevent it from being manipulated by a hack. It is more a matter of whether the Fed builds their own or uses an existing one. In either case, the digital dollar is unlikely to be decentralized the way Bitcoin and many other cryptos are.

Again, turning to China's digital yuan as an example, it is centralized, manipulated, and controlled by the People's Bank of China, just like real currency yuan. As DiMartino Booth said, "They've got a banking system that they can run at gunpoint."[6] So although technically digital yuan is a cryptocurrency, it is a centralized one, meaning it does not adhere to the ethos of most cryptos out there. The technology is the same; the application is different.

So back to the Fed's options. Ripple's system—which we discussed in the chapter on altcoins—is lightning fast. They have been a strong competitor to the traditional wire banking system and the SWIFT

---

6   Brandon Zemp, "Danielle DiMartino Booth: CEO of Quill Intelligence," *BlockHash: Exploring the Blockchain*, August 19, 2020, Spotify, 00:22:14, https://www.blockhash-podcast.com/podcast/danielle-dimartino-booth-ceo-of-quill-intelligence.

system. So people have discussed using Ripple's platform to build a CBDC or digital dollar and incorporate it into the banking system to use for remittances. But Ripple has been fighting a lawsuit by the SEC for several years now. The legal battles surrounding Ripple have sidelined much of the talk around using it to host a US CBDC.

The Federal Reserve is also interested in the Hedera Hashgraph (HBAR) system, which is fast and powerful. As we discussed, it is not a blockchain per se, but it is similar—another protocol of monetary consensus. As a reminder, HBAR has some of the biggest partnerships in the fintech space: Google, IBM, LG, Boeing, and others. They also got a lot of good press during the pandemic when healthcare systems started using their technology to track and monitor storage and delivery of temperature-sensitive COVID-19 vaccines. And they have been working with a company called Mtech Global to create a digital cash structure, which could be an option for the Fed.

The Future of the Dollar

The dollar is inflating each year at a fairly predictable rate. I like to explain inflation with what I call the cereal box theory. When I was a kid and I would buy a box of cereal, I would get a full box for $2.50, and the bag would be filled to the brim with Lucky Charms or Cocoa Puffs or whatever. Now, ten or fifteen years on, when I buy cereal, it costs me $5.00 a box, and the bag is only half-full!

That's inflation. The same box costs more and has less cereal. Why?

Instead of raising prices to deliver the same product, many companies just change or minimize the product they put out to keep the price artificially the same, and people don't freak out because they simply don't realize the change. In other words, companies incrementally increase price or decrease product content—or both—at an infinitesimal rate so that it is barely noticeable. Like the proverbial frog in a boiling pot, we don't know what's happening until we're dead in the water.

That's happening in our economy. Prices are rising, and we as consumers are losing purchasing power. And I think the breaking point will not be when the debt is too high or the dollar becomes worthless. It will happen when people realize there is not enough cereal in the box to feed themselves. It will be at that point, when people's livelihoods or comfort become affected, that things reach a crisis point.

We have seen it time and again—the fallout of hyperinflation—in the Weimar Republic, Zimbabwe, and Venezuela. The list goes on. The currency is no longer a trusted store of value subjectively, and there is nothing to give it value objectively. A country's currency is crushed and rendered useless, and as a result ordinary people can't afford to buy even essential goods.

Another chronic issue with the dollar is that, like anything, small inefficiencies at scale add up.

To get a better understanding of what I mean by "at scale," let's take a look at Amazon. It is $12.99 a month for a Prime membership, and with that you get lots of benefits—free movies and music, two-day shipping, and other special deals. Well, Amazon has millions of users paying that fairly nominal fee, so the company can afford to offer a lot of seemingly generous incentives.

The inefficiencies with analog dollars are small in simple transactions, but scale it up to more than 330 million people engaging in countless transactions. How many times a day do you swipe your card or pay a tab with cash? And a slow or inefficient system creates bottlenecks. Latency issues at scale can stymie economies. That's true for businesses as well, which often face cash flow problems that could be alleviated by a faster, more secure system.

So how do we get ourselves out of the boiling pot of water before it's too late? We know we must move out of this debt-paralyzed, unstable system. But how? I think the way forward will be through CBDCs or, preferably, a decentralized system that belongs to the people, like Bitcoin. Those are two opposing routes out of this system. I know which way I would go. In any event, a showdown is on the horizon. We will reach a fork in the road. And we must choose and prepare ourselves for a major shift in monetary policy before the system itself collapses.

A Debt Jubilee

Part of the reason governments are looking to make the shift toward CBDCs is because we finally have a viable alternative to fiat and the technology to make the move through blockchain. But I think an underlying motive for countries moving to CBDC is not so much its efficiency or because they want more control over monetary systems but because there is a huge debt bubble brewing in the US and globally. Many governments are in serious debt, in part because of fractional reserve banking, lending, inflating currency bases, and other ways they have handled—or mishandled—their obligations around monetary policy.

In the US there has been a persistent debate around quantitative easing, quantitative tightening, and the debt ceiling. According to DiMartino Booth, any hint of tightening is often enough to send the markets into a tailspin because we are so accustomed to artificial easing manipulated by the Fed. And the US debt is staggering. As of this writing, it was a whopping $28.8 *trillion*,[7] and it will probably never be paid off, but does that mean the US could one day default, triggering economic collapse?

Here is where the idea of a debt jubilee comes in. Debt is tied to the current monetary base. If you have one US dollar, it is equal to a certain amount of debt in dollars. If you wipe out the debt, you wipe out part of the monetary base. You can't raise or lower one without the other—a nasty correlation between debt and the value of your dollar. A debt jubilee means you cancel out all this debt, but to do so requires moving to a new monetary system.

So let's say the Federal Reserve releases a new digital dollar. You have ten years to take your old USD and exchange it for digital USD, one to one. When you "burn" that old dollar in the monetary supply, you are also erasing the corresponding debt. And that is one way to exit an indebted monetary system and achieve a "reset." A big caveat for it to work is that you would need other countries, say all the G20 countries, to agree to the same, so that everyone is on some kind of coordinated CBDC monetary system. Basically they cancel out each other's debt.

I personally think that may be the course of action governments are looking at. It is probably the only way to erase all that interlocking debt; otherwise, we face the prospect of a major global recession or an even more devastating protracted depression.

We caught a glimpse of what might happen in such a case with COVID-19—businesses grind to a halt, supply chains get disrupted, and things fall apart. Our economy is weaker than it seems because a

---

[7] "US National Debt Clock: Real Time," October 6, 2021, https://www.usdebtclock.org.

lot of it is predicated on this debt bubble. A CBDC provides an exit strategy.

Ultimately I do not think a debt jubilee using CBDC would be a good thing, but it might be the only option, in the minds of governing bodies, for maintaining economic stability. A brand-new Bretton Woods for the twenty-first century. And, if it gives you any piece of mind, DiMartino Booth, whose career is built on erudite, objective analysis of the Fed and its inner workings, believes the Fed is in good hands with Jerome Powell despite the looming debt crisis.

Surveillance and CBDCs

If you make a transaction with anything but cash, technically everything is reported. If you swipe a credit card or send a wire transfer, your bank records that transaction. And some people still like cash for that reason—it's not tracked. I live in Colombia, and people like cash transactions because, I hate to say it, it helps them avoid taxes. Obviously you should pay your taxes, but I do understand why some people want to avoid it. If I give you a buck and you give me a soda, there's no record. That vests a lot of freedom in purchasing power.

Now with credit and debit cards, there is a paper trail, but banks do not generally question individual transactions, unless there is something markedly suspicious—a purchase above your usual threshold or made from an unusual location. For example, I sometimes send money to Colombia, my bank asks *What's up with this?*, I approve the transaction, and it's all good. They are not particularly interested in what I'm doing with money because that information has little to no value to the bank. I don't like banks generally speaking. But can the government rely on a bank to get accurate information? Is the bank keeping a good record? How banks label transactions can vary greatly.

With blockchain, every transaction is reported. When you move to a digital currency based on blockchain, every transaction is recorded on the ledger, forever. With a blockchain like Bitcoin, there is no central or single entity, individual, or government sitting at the helm; it's decentralized, like we've talked about.

But if your money is a CBDC, then your money is no longer private, everything is surveilled, and powerful actors—state and nonstate—could use it as leverage against you. Imagine if your paycheck were held over your head or withheld unless you did XYZ? In the case of a CBDC, if I buy a soda, the government can know exactly when that purchase was made, from whom, for how much—every detail of the transaction. And if they really wanted, they could push a button, freeze my assets, and prevent me from using my own money. That is a dire risk to freedom.

And maybe you don't want the government to know you're spending fifty dollars a month on Pornhub or some other private or embarrassing thing. But beyond that, there are strong arguments for protecting privacy in general even if you're doing nothing "wrong." Do you want every aspect of your economic activity to be public?

This is the basic downfall of a cashless society: the capital controls that are thereby levied on citizens. Governments can end up dictating behaviors because of the financial leverage they hold over basically everyone. Do you get your subsidy or universal basic income check? Will your paycheck get auto-deducted for civil penalties (like a parking ticket or jaywalking)? If you forget to make a monthly rent payment, will your wages be auto-garnished? Will you be allowed to send money anywhere you like for any reason? Could your money be more easily frozen or seized based on arbitrary judgment? If you think that sounds extreme, there are already examples of US citizens having their Venmo payments to friends for things like "Cuban sandwich" or "Persian restaurant" being blocked because Venmo wrongly flags these transactions as in breach of US sanctions against Cuba and Iran.

When you live in a cashless society, where the money is completely controlled by the government or a central body, then you risk losing basic freedoms and liberties. That said, there is no reason to protect cash as a store of value. The original goal of cash was to create currency, a medium of exchange for money that couldn't easily be exchanged (such as gold). Since cryptocurrencies are seamless and easy to move, they eliminate the need for a medium of exchange and thus eliminate the necessity to have cash. CBDCs would accomplish the same goal, although in a centralized fashion.

Needless to say, it's a sticky situation. Even if we opt not to go the CBDC route in the US, other countries will, and that might hurt us economically in a digital world. Most things are thoroughly digitized now, but in ten years it will be even more so. Every industry and activity will be changed. A digital marketplace version of every niche industry out there will emerge, and that future necessitates a digital monetary system.

So to return to the example of China and the digital yuan, if their system is more efficient than, say, using paper dollars to pay for purchases, where does that leave the US in the global economy? And what does that future look like for financial and social freedom? We live in a globalized world. It will not be solely Chinese citizens using and trading in digital yuan. China is a huge trading partner for the rest of the world, and their reach is increasing with projects like the Belt and Road Initiative. And ultimately, China is run by an authoritarian government, and that has real implications.

China is already functionally cashless. If you pay with regular RMB, you do it with an app, usually Alipay or WeChat. You can go to any rural village and buy a two kuai ice cream by scanning a

QR code with your phone. Or pay your rent. Or earn a salary paid through one of these apps. Almost no one uses credit or debit cards. A lot of that stems from the fact that China was an early adopter of smartphones because, well, imagine trying to type a text message using the old T9 format of flip phones in a language that uses more than eighty thousand characters. It doesn't work. So you have nearly 1.5 billion people already using the same basic technology. All of that is to say, China is in a position to make an easier transition to a CBDC. In the US we are just starting to get to that point. We still depend on our credit cards, and we still use cash.

For Chinese citizens, a CBDC is not necessarily a big change on the surface, but it gives the government even more oversight and control. The Chinese government already monitors WeChat chat groups and financial transactions, but those, unlike exchanges through their DCEP, can be deleted or hidden. The permanence of the digital ledger of transactions with blockchains is a double-edged sword. Like so much technology, it can change the world for better or worse, depending on who wields it. In many ways, China has traded technological advancement for individual freedom. Obviously it is a different system from what we have in the US, which means that their CBDC is not necessarily a typical case study.

And I want to take a moment to point out that, yes, a lot of this discussion is positioned from a Western standpoint where we value our civil liberties, and we live in an economically free capitalist society. And we look at China and think, "That's awful." And I'm inclined to agree. That said, in Eastern society, they have different values and ethics. Many of the citizens there are willing to give up certain freedoms we feel are inviolable in the US because doing so grants them other benefits or because they have little power to do otherwise. For example, if you are a good, law-abiding citizen and you do well at your job, then you will have good social credit and reap the benefits, like low-interest loans, job security, and economic comfort. And that is not to say that there are not elements within China that rebel against the status quo, and it goes without saying that the people of a country are not the same as their government, all the more so in an authoritarian context.

So I think it is important to temper our condemnation of other systems by acknowledging our cultural biases, especially with respect to what we value versus what others value. Everything, really, is a trade-off. We all make complicated personal calculations on how we prioritize freedoms, wants, and desires.

The real question as I see it is whether or not we will live in a society where finance remains centralized or becomes decentralized. The best outcome in my view is to use cryptocurrency and have a decentralized monetary system. Then you have the benefit of being cashless while also retaining your freedoms and liberties.

An alternative to issuing a CBDC and a solution to the problem of government surveillance is for a country to make Bitcoin legal tender. El Salvador did it. Politicians in a number of other Latin American countries have expressed interest in following suit—in large part as a means of dealing with skyrocketing inflation. Ukraine recently passed a law that legalizes and regulates cryptocurrency, but they have also indicated that they are modernizing their systems to enable the issuance of digital currency. I imagine by the time you read this that many other countries will have joined the parade.

If a CBDC is the most centralized currency, Bitcoin is the decentralized competitor.

So that's CBDCs in a nutshell. One of the big questions in CBDCs is how monetary policy can affect them, but what about decentralized cryptos? Given all the possibilities out there, how do different tokens function in their economic environment? Why does it matter? Up next, we will answer exactly those questions.

CHAPTER 8
TOKENOMICS

Cryptocurrencies are revolutionizing economics through tokenomics. We have touched on this term before. Tokenomics is a portmanteau of tokens and economics, as you might have already deduced. It is a recent term that was coined when developers started issuing tokens on blockchains, and that meant they had to determine an economic model for each token. It is a bit like a central bank implementing monetary policy to regulate its currency. Without some kind of governing rules, a cryptocurrency (or any currency) would likely fail.

So, simply put, tokenomics refers to the economics of a crypto token. It accounts for four basic features: the allocation and distribution of a token, the supply of tokens, the market cap, and the actual token model or how it works in an ecosystem of cryptos. When a new token is created, the developers or founders will generally issue a white paper explaining the whats and whys of their particular tokenomics.

The easiest way to understand tokenomics is to look at some examples. Let's break down the tokenomic models of bitcoin and ether using those four basic features.

The Tokenomics of Bitcoin

First, how is bitcoin allocated and distributed? Bitcoin is based on proof of work, as we discussed earlier. Each time a block is placed on the blockchain—which happens roughly every ten minutes, or 144 blocks per day—6.25 bitcoins are awarded to the miners and the network in exchange for their computational efforts. So all of the bitcoin in existence has been distributed through mining. The number of bitcoins awarded per block is cut in half every four years in a process known colloquially as halving. And that four-year period equates to 210,000 blocks on the blockchain, give or take. Right now, about 900 bitcoins are mined daily, or roughly 328,500 annually.[8] The next halving will take place in 2024, and the bitcoin award will drop to 3.125 BTC per mined block.

There is a maximum supply of twenty-one million bitcoins, and 90 percent of that supply is already in circulation. That limit is crucial to the economic model of Bitcoin and whether it's an inflationary or deflationary model. The final bitcoin will be mined in 2140. So we still have a long time before the total supply is in circulation. But what this means is that Bitcoin has an inflationary model that decreases over time. This differs from most fiat economic models, which are inflationary by design to keep people from hoarding currency (though some people don't seem to have gotten the message).

As for its market cap, that's sitting pretty at over $1 trillion. It's crazy. To put that in context, there are hundreds of stock exchanges around the world—the New York Stock Exchange and NASDAQ are probably the most familiar. Almost every country has its own stock exchange or multiple stock exchanges. Of the hundreds that exist, only sixteen have a market cap over $1 trillion. And there are only a handful of companies globally that have hit that mark.

---

[8] Buy Bitcoin Worldwide, "How Many Bitcoins Are There?" February, 1 2022, https://www.buybitcoinworldwide.com/how-many-bitcoins-are-there/.

The big takeaway for this tokenomics model is the fact that there is a finite amount of bitcoin that can ever come into circulation—twenty-one million—and you can never create more bitcoin. That number can never change. It is set in stone forever. And the inflation rate decreases every four years or so when the block reward gets cut in half. So Bitcoin's tokenomics functionally stymies its own ability to inflate in price unchecked and become worthless at any point in time. In fact, Bitcoin's model actually helps achieve the opposite; it helps bitcoins increase in price, which is a strength. It makes Bitcoin a relatively reliable investment over the long term because it is somewhat more predictable compared to most speculative investment options.

> There is a finite amount of bitcoin that can ever come into circulation—twenty-one million—and you can never create more bitcoin.

Now a quick aside: Yes, Bitcoin is a speculative asset. I can't argue against that because it is very volatile, but over time its tokenomics model has proven to be solid. Since its start in 2009, the price has done nothing but increase in value. Of course, if you are day-trading bitcoin, you will have a different view of its volatility. But long term, I think its tokenomics make it a sound asset. It is also elegantly simple compared to other tokenomics or even the economic models of many fiat currencies, which can be staggeringly complex. And that simplicity makes Bitcoin more effective as a currency because people understand it better.

The Tokenomics of Ethereum

Ethereum is more complex than Bitcoin but similar in some respects. Unlike Bitcoin, when Ethereum came out, the creators distributed seventy-two million pre-mined ether to investors, contributors, and the Ethereum Foundation. This is known as the genesis supply, and it makes up the majority of ether in circulation. Interestingly, ether does not have a maximum supply (although there have been proposals to cap it, even from Vitalik Buterin). That sounds bad on paper, but other aspects of its tokenomics model correct for this.

So while technically its supply is unlimited, there is a limited amount that can come into circulation each year—roughly eighteen million ether. That limit functions as a built-in, slow inflation rate. There are about 117 million ether circulating globally now. The Ethereum network is designed to produce a block every twelve seconds (compared to Bitcoin's ten minutes!), and miners are awarded two ether per block. On average, only about five million come into circulation annually, which is far less than the maximum allowed by its tokenomics.

Another failsafe is that a certain amount of ether gets burned, which is just to say it gets removed from the protocol and taken out of circulation. It effectively no longer exists. When a transaction is made on the Ethereum blockchain—say you buy an NFT or run a smart contract, for example—a portion of the transaction fees gets burned from circulation. About 2.6 million ether are removed from circulation annually at the present rate. So that guards against an oversupply of ether, which would devalue it (a basic principle of supply and demand). In this sense, it, like Bitcoin, obeys an inflationary model that decreases over time. And the more people who use Ethereum, the more transactions there are and the greater the fees, then the more tokens get burned. So it could even change from an inflationary model to a deflationary model if more tokens are being burned than come into circulation, which may well happen as Ethereum and its various applications become more widely adopted.

Another distinguishing factor is that Ethereum's tokenomics are somewhat more dynamic than Bitcoin's. There have already been updates to address issues like transaction price volatility, network efficiency, and scalability.

Furthermore, as we have discussed, the Ethereum Foundation's goal is to change to a more complex tokenomics model commonly known as Ethereum 2.0. They want to shift from proof of work to proof of stake. With proof of stake, people can lock ether into the network and earn "yields" on that, much like interest in a checking account. This has other benefits such as deterring selling (because people hold on to it) and curbing volatility. In fact, the option to stake your ether and participate in that model is already available, but the two blockchains, old and new, have yet to be merged. So while you can stake Ethereum 2.0, right now, it's a bit like *Field of Dreams*. If you stake it, they will come. It's just that Ethereum 2.0 hasn't stepped out of the cornfields and onto the diamond yet.

Tokenomics versus Economics

So how do these tokenomic models stack up against traditional economic models? Let's take the US dollar as our prime example. The economics of the dollar is fraught with issues. The Federal Reserve is constantly having to issue more USD. We just raised the debt ceiling *again*, which we do every few years. We have a fractional reserve banking system, meaning the bank that holds your money can loan out 90 percent of every dollar you deposit, and this bank credit inflates the monetary base, leading to more debt in the system than actual money to pay it down. And that debt cannot be paid down without wiping out a portion of the monetary base.

As we touched on in the last chapter, the Federal Reserve and Congress are largely to blame for this. Combine that with the choice to move the dollar from the gold standard in the 1970s, when every dollar was backed by an equivalent store of gold, and here we are today.

Now the US dollar, like many other fiat currencies, has major inflationary and debt concerns as a result of these poor economic models. If we do nothing about it and let the debt spiral out of control, we could face hyperinflation where the almighty dollar becomes worthless (as has happened in Venezuela, Zimbabwe, Argentina, and other infamous examples). Even if governments could pay down their debt, they would be cutting into their monetary supply, which in turn could trigger a deflationary recession or depression.

It's something of a quagmire, but it highlights the hidden (or not so hidden) precarity of most economies, including developed ones. To explore this, we can look at the European counterpart to the Federal Reserve: The European Central Bank (ECB). Its current president, Christine Lagarde, is also the former managing director of the International Monetary Fund (IMF). She is the first woman to become finance minister of a G8 economy (France, in her case) and the first woman to head both the ECB and the IMF. So she's got major chops when it comes to economics and economic policy. And she has been making decisions that contrast sharply to those of the Federal Reserve, especially in relation to inflation.

Unlike the Fed and a host of other Western central banks, Lagarde does not believe in implementing tighter monetary policies in response to skyrocketing inflation rates. She has set an inflation goal for the ECB of 2 percent or below.[9] (In comparison, in the latest Labor Department report, the US consumer price index rose by 5.4 percent compared to the previous year.[10]) She argues that positive inflation can help balance economies.

Interestingly, she has also come out in favor of CBDCs. While she has been clear that she does not believe cryptocurrencies are currencies, and she takes issue with what she sees as its vulnerabilities to criminal misuse, she has acknowledged the utility of other blockchain-based tools like CBDCs and stablecoins (asset-backed cryptos) in the face of an increasingly digital world.

Tokenomics can teach us about alternatives and viable solutions that governments could apply if they were to use blockchain. Even the head of the ECB has something to learn from them! In contrast to fiat currency, the tokenomics of a crypto token are implemented through software code. Issue rates and schedules are predetermined, which makes them more predictable than fiat currency (we never know when the Fed will decide to print more money or how much). Even burn rates are fairly predictable, as we saw with the example of Ethereum. And that predictability translates into transparency for investors.

It is possible to move to a better currency, a more transparent system, a sounder economic structure, and grant consumers more control over debt, increase GDP, and eliminate the need for red tape and regulations.

---

9   Christine Lagarde, "The Monetary Policy Review: Some Preliminary Considerations," ECB and Its Watchers XXI Conference, Frankfurt am Main, September 30 2020.

10   Gwynn Guilford, "Accelerating Inflation Spreads through the Economy," *The Wall Street Journal,* October 13, 2021.

Alternative Tokenomic Models

As we know, there are a multitude of blockchains out there, and virtually every one of them has an associated token and therefore must have a tokenomic model. Most use similar models to Bitcoin or Ethereum. The biggest differentiator between tokenomic models is probably between proof of work and proof of stake. Some blockchains have designed complicated structures for bringing tokens into circulation or burning tokens based on a litany of factors.

If I designed my own tokenomics, I would use one similar or identical to Bitcoin. Why? Because Bitcoin has been successful. It has steadily gone up in value—in spite of its volatility. Its value has been largely consistent. It has never gone offline. Its tokenomics model has never been changed or broken. And it is simple and easy to understand. There really is not much to criticize or change. And if it ain't broke, don't fix it. Ultimately, Bitcoin's tokenomics is a potent example of a decentralized economic model that people—and governments—can use.

Bitcoin's tokenomics is a potent example of a decentralized economic model that people—and governments—can use.

Next up, we will look at the world of blockchain beyond cryptocurrencies. We know that it can and has revolutionized investing and economics. What else can it do? How else is the technology being applied? And where else might it be headed?

CHAPTER 9
DeFi DEMYSTIFIED

We have spent a lot of time looking at crypto; now I want to get into the wider world of blockchain and what it can do. Since we've gone in depth with cryptocurrencies, a good place to start is with blockchain applications most closely associated with finance: decentralized finance, or DeFi, as it is known.

Decentralized finance is an umbrella term for a cornucopia of applications and projects in the blockchain space. In some ways, it is easiest to define DeFi by what it isn't, because DeFi is mostly geared toward the idea of disrupting traditional finance, or TradFi, which relies on banks, brokers, lenders, creditors, custodians, or other intermediaries to manage money and assets. It includes financial tools like investment or equity finance (selling part of your business for cash), loans, grants, and overdrafts (to bridge gaps in cash flow). TradFi is also synonymous with the failure to realize risk in the economy and poor decisions that lead to economic problems like the 2008 recession, caused by reckless lending, among other things. Another element of TradFi and an area ripe for critique is the fact that TradFi requires the user to relinquish control and information, sometimes putting up collateral or signing away certain rights as terms for securing a loan.

In contrast, DeFi does not require any type of access or rights to use them in the way TradFi does, even for things like lending and borrowing. It is a very open system in comparison.

Another term that's important to understand in this discussion is centralized finance, or CeFi. Centralized finance is like the TradFi version of blockchain. While it allows people easy access to do things like trade and loan cryptocurrencies, it comes with strings attached. Centralized exchanges like Binance and Coinbase require users to undergo verification steps, including anti-money laundering (AML) and know your customer (KYC), which means that transactions are not anonymous, and the platform holds the private keys to your crypto holdings. It undermines individual authority and control, and the people running the financial system already have a lot of control over you and what you do with your money. To me, this negates one of the primary principles of what makes blockchain such a revolutionary technology.

So back to DeFi. When Ethereum launched in 2015, it kicked off the dialogue about whether decentralized finance was possible. With Ethereum's introduction of smart contracts, that possibility came one step nearer reality, since the whole point of DeFi is to elide the intermediary or middleman in the process. Then MakerDAO took on the challenge. It launched one of the first protocols for creating a decentralized stablecoin, DAI. Originally, it only accepted ether as collateral for loans but has since expanded. EtherDelta was another early, if short lived, iteration of DeFi; it's now defunct after being hacked in 2017.

In the years since, countless products and projects have emerged in the wake of those initial DeFi projects—like Aave, REN, Kyber, Compound, Yearn Finance, the list goes on. There was a real rise in popularity in 2020. We've seen terms like "DeFi summer" ascribed to the summers of 2020 and 2021, when DeFi blew up. Its notoriety testified to its growth. Billions of dollars of investment have since flowed into DeFi projects. People are excited about the possibility of low-fee, frictionless, transparent alternatives to traditional finance.

Just how successful is DeFi, and how is that measured? Total value locked (TVL) is the standard metric for how much money is deposited in DeFi. And it is worth noting that TVL can vary pretty widely based on a service's algorithm, listing times, and other factors in their calculation. For instance, today, the TVL in DeFi is $106.58 billion according to DeFi Pulse,[11] $194.64 billion according to CoinGecko,[12] and $247.03 billion on DefiLlama.[13] (By comparison, those same sites list the TVL at the end of 2020 between $20 and $25 billion. How's that for growth?) But any way you slice it, it's a tremendous piece of the pie.

In fall 2021, I spoke with Rafael Cosman on the subject of DeFi. Cosman is the CEO and cofounder of TrustToken, the creators of the world's first compliant, independently attested digital dollar, TrueUSD, along with other global, fiat-backed stablecoins. He's also a Stanford graduate and former member of the Google Brain team. In 2020, TrustToken launched TrueFi, which is their DeFi protocol for uncollateralized lending. His vision is to build open financial infrastructure to help empower people and give them control of their assets. As he says, "What the internet did for information, we think blockchain is doing for money."[14]

---

[11] DeFi Pulse, "Total Value Locked (USD) in DeFi," October 29, 2021, www.defipulse.com.

[12] CoinGecko, "Top 100 DeFi Coins by Market Capitalization," October 29, 2021, https://www.coingecko.com/en/categories/decentralized-finance-defi.

[13] DefiLlama, "Defi Dashboard," October 29, 2021, www.defillama.com.

[14] Brandon Zemp, "Rafael Cosman: CEO of TrustToken," *BlockHash: Exploring the Blockchain*, October 20, 2021, Spotify, 00:05:05, https://www.blockhashpodcast.com/podcast/rafael-cosman-of-trusttoken.

And that's the real drive behind DeFi. It is a way to get more advanced financial tools into the hands of everyone without the restrictions and red tape of traditional finance. It's a democratic, open, fast, transparent means of lending and borrowing, and in many cases, it's essentially borderless. For example, with TrueFi you can send USD-backed stablecoins across the globe in seconds. And with DeFi holdings generally, you can see in real time how every penny of your investments is used and why, and you get better returns on your investment.

So what does all this mean for you? What is DeFi being used for, and how can you get involved in the space?

DeFi in the Real World

DeFi gives ordinary people direct access to financial tools and services, no banks or brokerages required. Need a loan to buy a new car? How about sending money to a friend or family member without the wait time of a wire transfer? Or maybe you're looking for a better way to invest your savings by earning higher annual percentage yield (APY) than your bank offers. What are your options when it comes to DeFi? There are four primary categories of transactions in DeFi: lending and borrowing, decentralized exchanges, stablecoins, and prediction markets.

1. LENDING AND BORROWING

DeFi allows individuals to borrow money at specific interest rates whenever they want without limitations based on credit rating, employment, or other history and background. That is hugely advantageous if you can't secure loans through traditional financial institutions, like a bank. It's more open. Most DeFi protocols require you to have collateral to do it—so you need some liquid assets—but that's the only real caveat.

One popular project is called Compound Finance, which was developed on Ethereum. It allows users to accrue interest by lending out crypto assets or borrow against collateral. You earn APY for lending, which can be really high, upwards of 8 to 12 percent on the year, which is striking compared to a traditional savings account at a bank whose interest is usually a tiny fraction of 1 percent.

So people are taking their money out of the bank and staking it on these protocols. Ten percent a year on a million dollars? That's $100,000 in interest for doing absolutely nothing.

Collateralized Borrowing

Borrowing with collateral is the most common way to borrow. In a TradFi model, you might borrow money from the bank using your house as collateral. In the DeFi world, say you have $1,000 in bitcoin and want to borrow against it. You can use the bitcoin as collateral to borrow a specific amount—usually as much as 50 percent, or up to $500 on your $1,000 worth of bitcoin. You can do this as long as you pay back the principal with interest (which is usually small). You can pay it back whenever you want; there is no timeline and no minimum fee.

If you do not pay back the loan, eventually you will lose all or part of your collateral, or the interest accrued on what you borrowed might be deducted to pay the principal. So it is in your interest (no pun intended) to pay back the loan. Of course, if the value of bitcoin rises over time, you will be able to pay down that loan with relative ease.

The risk is if you borrow in bitcoin and bitcoin goes down in value, the lender may take your collateral to pay for it. It is not a risk-free financial tool, but it is useful and widely accessible.

Uncollateralized Borrowing

Uncollateralized loans also exist, and it is as straightforward as it sounds. TrueFi, which I mentioned earlier, was the first to offer uncollateralized borrowing options for vetted users. Aave is another protocol offering what they call flash loans, which do not require collateral. Borrow what you need, pay back the principal and interest, and any fees collected go back into the liquidity pool for further lending.

Eventually DeFi can give you a decentralized credit score attached to your wallet, and you can use that to show your likelihood of paying back a loan, how much you hold or trade—in other words, your creditworthiness.

2. DECENTRALIZED EXCHANGES

These are also called dexes, and they are an essential function of DeFi. They allow users to exchange or swap tokens, crypto, or other digital assets without having to use a centralized intermediary, custodian, or exchange. Traditional exchanges have basically the same offerings, but they are subject to the exchange's costs, fees, background checks, identification methods, vetting process, jurisdictional restrictions—a lot of roadblocks that can hold you back from taking advantage of an exchange.

A dex is a place where anyone can go and trade however and whenever they want without the friction of a traditional exchange. Naturally, this raises an ethical debate. But in a world where privacy is rare and access is centralized, it has its benefits.

One popular dex is Uniswap, the largest automated token exchange in the world by volume. Uniswap automates transactions between different cryptocurrencies via smart contract, so you do not need an intermediary to facilitate it. The protocol runs the exchange all on its own. Other exchanges like Uniswap have emerged, too. And the increase in competition means that these platforms have gotten rather cheap in terms of fees.

It helps that dexes are easy to access. Visit the site in your browser, connect your wallet, and that's it. You can start trading. There is no onboarding, registration, or verification required.

3. STABLECOINS

Stablecoins are a simple concept. They are cryptos pegged to fiat currency like the dollar. Tether is the most well-known, but TrueUSD, which we've talked about, is another one gaining momentum. Stablecoins don't have to be tied to USD. They could be tied to the price of gold, commodities, or other fiat currencies. TrustToken has launched stablecoins in British pounds, Canadian dollars, Australian dollars, and Hong Kong dollars. The idea is to create cryptos pegged to the value of "real-world" assets that do not change. This makes it an effective trading instrument because it serves as a good medium of flow.

MakerDAO is another major player on this front. It is an organization that builds out technology for savings, borrowing, lending, and other crypto projects built on Ethereum. Their main product is DAI, a stablecoin that is tied to the US dollar, one to one like Tether, but it works more seamlessly in the Ethereum ecosystem. DAI can be integrated with any smart contract on the Ethereum network, so whether you are selling an NFT or executing a smart contract, you could easily convert ether to DAI and then manage your money in USD, which may be easier conceptually for investors and traders.

4. PREDICTION MARKETS

Prediction markets have not received much attention yet, but they have massive potential. Prediction markets allow individuals to make predictions on future events like sports betting, politics or elections, stock prices—anything with variable outcomes, really. They can also be used for research, gambling, polling, and even voting processes. I expect it to gain traction in the DeFi world.

Augur is a decentralized prediction market protocol that utilizes the collective predictions of the masses. They have been around since 2015, which makes them ancient in crypto terms.

It is an Ethereum-based protocol, so you can bid ether on a yes/no question-and-answer scheme—something as simple as "Which team will win? Baltimore Ravens vs. Seattle Seahawks." You can make money (by gambling), but you can also use it solely as a polling or feedback tool. Finance.vote, for instance, introduced a dapp called markets.vote that offers quadratic voting, wherein participants vote for or against an issue or candidate *and* can express how strongly they feel about it.

There are not many use cases for it yet, but it will likely expand in prominence.

But if you can do all or most of these things through a traditional financial institution, what's the big deal? A big difference between DeFi and TradFi is that the fees accrued from the money being staked, borrowed, or lent stay within that pool, within the protocol, and go back toward rewarding people for using the platform—instead of being siphoned off to executives or shareholders.

As Cosman pointed out in our interview, it's not because banks are loaning your money at 0.1 percent that you receive 0.1 percent APY on your savings account; it is because the profits from lending go to shareholders and managers. Banks are using your money to make themselves richer. With traditional banking, you put a buck in your bank account, that bank can loan out 90 percent of your dollar (according to fractional banking law) at, say, a 3 to 5 percent interest rate. So when you deposit a dollar, only ten cents are actually in your account. Ninety cents are being loaned to make money—for the bank, not you. (The real kicker is that many banks charge fees on top of that—for opening an account, maintaining an account, withdrawing money, using an ATM, going into overdraft, overseas purchases, wire transfers—the list goes on.)

But banks can't give you a higher yield without potentially collapsing the whole system because there is so much debt that must be paid off. When the chairman of the Fed comes on TV and starts talking about raising interest rates, it can seem very abstract, but it does materially affect the average person. When you have lower interest rates, it is easier to borrow money because the bank does not have to pay back all that money they borrowed. Raising interest rates is better for savers than for folks who want to borrow, since savers earn more in interest.

DeFi doesn't suffer from the broken, overly complex rules that define TradFi. In DeFi, that system does not exist. The money stays within these protocols. Fees go to people lending, borrowing, and putting up collateral on the platforms. Obviously the high APYs are attracting users, and the more users, the more liquidity, and the better the service is in the long run.

The Tether Controversy

There are legitimate questions to be asked about decentralized finance and what protections it offers to investors and borrowers. Regulators went after Tether in what became a protracted lawsuit because they suspected Tether did not have the necessary reserves of USD, contrary to the company's continued claims and official attestation. Since a stablecoin in theory can be redeemed for its corresponding asset at any time, any platform that deals in stablecoins must have the corresponding reserves. In other words, if someone owns one tether, they should be able to redeem it for one dollar.

Authorities have been poking and prodding at Tether, which has shown that they do have a set of reserves in dollars, but the findings still land in a kind of gray area. What do they actually have? Is Tether fudging the numbers? Are the regulators full of shit?

Whatever the truth is, they reached a settlement. Tether will pay $41 million to the US Commodity Futures Trading Commission (CFTC) for misleading statements. As a result of a separate lawsuit with the New York attorney general, Tether can no longer do business in the state of New York, the financial center of the US. And *still* Tether remains the biggest stablecoin on the market.

But this controversy sparked a bigger debate. Must stablecoins be backed one to one? I would counter that by asking, *Is the dollar backed by anything?* Governments don't like stablecoins because they are basically a digital version of the dollar, and governments don't want something competing with their own sovereign currency (not to mention future CBDCs).

Personally, I think the point of the space is to push back against everything that is centralized and give us options and choices. I don't like the idea of stifling innovation. We are still in the early days of the industry. I am more interested in seeing innovation, even if it can be messy or chaotic at times. We need it all the more now because the finance industry has severely lacked innovation, especially technological innovation. And DeFi offers us great hope for a better, sounder financial system. So if I had to pick sides, I would side with Tether.

Let the market decide if Tether succeeds or fails. That said, if they make promises that people can redeem in dollars, they should fulfill those promises.

Risks and Regulations

Any technology that is brand new, innovative, and disruptive will always face pushback, and there will always be drawbacks and risks. Imagine being a villager when mechanical clocks were introduced, and now you have to be at a certain place at a certain "time," when that concept didn't even exist for you the week before. No thank you. But those adjustments are part and parcel of the process of creating something new, of advancing. There will always be something to fix or improve upon.

In DeFi, one issue is making sure that there is sufficient liquidity to offer these services. This prevents large shareholders (whales) from manipulating the value of a particular asset and ensures that investors can easily convert cryptos into cash.

> **Any technology that is brand new, innovative, and disruptive will always face pushback, and there will always be drawbacks and risks.**

In traditional finance, if a bank goes under, the Federal Deposit Insurance Corporation (FDIC) will reimburse depositors up to a certain amount. No such failsafe exists as yet in the DeFi space.

Collateralization also comes with a degree of risk. For example, anyone can get a loan for any purpose. That's great. That's going to open a lot of doors for a lot of people. But if you borrow at the wrong time and crypto prices tank, you might lose your collateralized crypto and potentially your means of paying back that loan. Not to mention that collateral can be an obstacle for some borrowers to begin with.

But these questions are being addressed and answered every day by innovators in the space.

As for regulation, governments are limited in what they can do in the space. Take Uniswap, for example. It is not a company per se. A regulator can't simply walk down to the headquarters on Main Street and padlock the doors. Sure, there is a creator, a team, managers, but it is all decentralized. A counterexample might be something like Silk Road, which was a dark web market where users could do things anonymously, and generally those things were illegal, like buying drugs or hiring hitmen. Silk Road existed on a single server, which meant it could be brought down relatively easily. And that is exactly what happened when the FBI arrested Ross Ulbricht in a San Francisco library. However, the protocol Silk Road ran on, the Onion Network, is totally decentralized. So while the FBI eliminated Silk Road, someone else could easily create a new dark web market on the same protocol, which was also exactly what happened, as there are now various Silk Road-like markets on the dark web.

Uniswap does not trade in anything illegal, but like the dark web, it is decentralized, and there's no easy way to bring it down, even if governments wanted to. It is more likely that governments will regulate and tax crypto and DeFi rather than try to destroy it. They can make more money by allowing and taxing it than by trying to suppress it. I imagine major financial institutions will eventually incorporate DeFi because it makes their model stronger. I wouldn't be surprised if Bank of America or Wells Fargo introduce a DeFi platform or even become DeFi banks.

The Future of DeFi

DeFi has grown exponentially in the last couple years. It has been like a quantum leap in finance. There are huge amounts of money moving into DeFi, and given how novel it is, it is pretty wild to watch happen. This has put TradFi markets and players on edge; they are afraid of losing their dominance or market share. But DeFi is on the cutting edge of innovation in an industry that has so long been lacking in it.

I think a major reason for DeFi's success is that people are sick and tired of how money is handled by traditional financial institutions. Banking can be a headache. You go to the bank and can't open an account because you didn't bring the right forms, or you checked off the wrong box on one of a dozen forms. Or you're denied a loan by the gatekeepers. Or bombarded with "rewards" and promotions or solicited for credit cards. New businesses often find it hard to get off the ground because they depend on closed-off institutions for financial support. And the technology powering the financial world is somewhat dated—that was actually one of the reasons Rafael Cosman started TrustToken: to address the technology deficit in estate planning. There hasn't been much innovation in the "financial rails" that move money around.

> **DeFi is on the cutting edge of innovation in an industry that has so long been lacking in it.**

DeFi is so much better, more efficient, and more profitable for ordinary consumers that it eliminates the need for much of traditional finance. Not to mention, its transparency means it is in many ways more secure, trustworthy, and auditable. Theoretically, I could use DeFi to replace every aspect of TradFi that I need to run my business, invest my assets, and make everyday transactions. And I believe that will become more and more prevalent for the average person, too. I hear stories all the time of how irksome, overbearing, or alienating TradFi can be for both consumers and businesses. So I think we all need to be braced for the showdown between traditional and centralized finance and decentralized finance. I think Cosman put it really well: "A certain amount of that kind of centralization is inevitable.... At the same time, I think we need to fight to preserve, we need to push to preserve the things that we value—decentralization, open protocols that treat people equally, etcetera."[15]

DeFi is still in its infancy. Cosman anticipates this becoming a trillion-dollar market in the next decade.[16] For my part, I think we'll see a further expansion with the (now much referenced) move to Ethereum 2.0, which will allow for more scalable DeFi projects. Going forward, I think we just need to ensure that fees stay low, that protocols remain fast and inclusive, and that they are interoperable so that you can use them wherever you go, across blockchains. It will without doubt reshape and rebuild financial systems and services in a major way. It may even be an invaluable tool in closing the wealth gap. It has helped advance blockchain, made it even more prominent, and introduced new use cases. Most importantly, it is going a long way toward helping realize the notion of a democratized financial system.

As we're learning, blockchain is fast becoming more than just a finance tool. In the next chapter, we will see what blockchain can do when it is unhitched from the financial sector.

---

15 Brandon Zemp, "Rafael Cosman: CEO of TrustToken."
16 Brandon Zemp, "Rafael Cosman: CEO of TrustToken."

CHAPTER 10
BLOCKCHAIN UNCHAINED

Cryptocurrency is only one application of blockchain technology. As we have touched on briefly in other chapters, blockchain can be applied in creative ways to revolutionize nearly every industry. Other than financial use cases, there are a host of industries that can use blockchain, and this chapter will highlight some of the most exciting ones. We will look at applications for music and arts, licensing and registration, voting systems, supply chain management, and anticounterfeiting.

Royalties

First off, blockchain has the potential to overhaul the way musicians and artists make money from their creative work. In the current setup, musicians often sell ownership of their music to a third party (usually a record label), and in exchange, they receive a small payment or royalty any time their music is played on the radio, streamed through a service, used in a TV show or movie, or performed at concerts or other venues. And this applies to other industries as well. People and businesses receive royalties for trademarks and patents, for example. Athletes might get royalties for the use of their name and likeness. But let's stick with music for the time being.

Take the dispute between Taylor Swift and Scooter Braun, which has been getting headlines lately. When Swift was starting out as a young artist, she signed away the rights to the master recordings of her first six albums in exchange for a cash advance to kickstart her career. She was only fifteen at the time. Then, in 2019, Scooter Braun bought the record label Big Machine that Swift originally recorded those albums with and, along with it, the rights to her recordings in a $300 million deal. The following year, Swift was notified that Braun had sold the rights on to an investment company, despite the fact that Swift was actively negotiating to buy the masters back herself. Swift never saw a penny of either sale—that's reportedly over $600 million in all—because she had no ownership over the masters, but Braun, according to the deal with Shamrock Holdings, will continue to profit off Swift's back catalog for years to come. Swift, meanwhile, has decided to rerecord all those albums in an attempt to regain control of her music. She is also helping jump-start an independent artist movement making money outside the studio system.

Swift's is perhaps the most visible case of an artist who has signed over her intellectual property to a big company, leading to major disputes down the line, but her case is the norm, not the exception, for the music industry—despite the fact that most would agree that the creator, the artist, deserves the lion's share of the profit for their work.

So what does this have to do with blockchain? Blockchain can have a massive impact on helping artists profit from their work and maintain ownership. Blockchain applications like smart contracts, decentralized autonomous organizations (DAOs), and NFTs empower artists to maintain ownership of their work or sell portions of their work while remaining a royalty owner and/or retaining publishing rights. It gives control back to the artist. And it makes sense in an era when most music is consumed digitally.

Mary Spio is the CEO of a company called CEEK. She started out as an aerospace engineer and eventually branched out into creating satellite-based technologies for the music industry. And like the rest of us, she started getting into blockchain, which leads us to her brainchild, CEEK. CEEK is a platform that combines streaming services, virtual reality, and blockchain. It empowers musicians, artists, athletes, and actors to independently make money on their work. That includes publishing music and music videos, distributing content, and engaging with fans more directly. As she sees it, the platform is a way to open up engagement away from limitations of event venues and bandwidth. A musician might sell out a concert venue, but how much of the money from that do they see? And how many of their fans miss out because there are only so many seats, or the venue is charging a fortune for tickets? As she says, "CEEK was created … to sell tickets to the 99 percent of music fans, of live event fans that are not able to attend events."[17] Now millions of users can simultaneously attend virtual reality concerts and sporting events on the platform.

Basically it provides an escape route from the reliance on big labels, production companies, and sports leagues and teams. Lady Gaga, Katy Perry, and Ringo Starr have all created content for the platform. And CEEK is growing quickly and using blockchain in creative ways. Imagine you're at that CEEK Lady Gaga performance. You can look around and make in-platform purchases using tokens for things like T-shirts and NFTs. For artists, blockchain authen-

---

17   Brandon Zemp, "Mary Spio: CEO of CEEK," *BlockHash: Exploring the Blockchain*, September 4, 2021, Spotify, 00:04:47, https://www.blockhashpodcast.com/podcast/mary-spio-of-ceek.

ticates and authorizes the number of tickets to each event or piece of content on the platform. This means that artists receive accurate royalties for their work, unlike other streaming services that can have discrepancies in those numbers. They also get royalties for those in-platform purchases. And CEEK uses smart contracts to automatically pay their artists every time a user streams their content or buys an NFT.

These applications and platforms are not a bad arrangement for record labels either. Record labels can offer more transparency and still make money. A smart contract—as compared to a hundred-page document—is generally more transparent and impartial and allows both parties to profit while minimizing the chance of one person taking advantage of the other. It can't be altered without the consent of both parties, and it holds up better in court, without the need for lawyers fighting over its meaning. And as an artist, you can create a contract without attorneys or without distributors or labels. It gives artists great flexibility and autonomy. It frees you of reliance on the tools and resources of a major label. And it means that record labels can more easily sign new artists, which diversifies their artist list. It cleans up the whole process.

This concept can be applied in other businesses that deal in royalties, trademarks, and patents, too.

Identification and Proof of Ownership

If you have ever stood in line for hours at the DMV waiting to get your driver's license renewed or spent weeks waiting for a new passport, hoping that it arrives before your big trip, then you will definitely like this next blockchain use case. Imagine instead of waiting in line or mailing off important, sensitive documents (which has always seemed crazy to me), you could just push a button and update your official ID.

Because blockchain creates a permanent, authenticated digital ledger, it is an ideal technology for anything to do with official documentation: titles for cars, real estate deeds, personal IDs, health records, business or professional licenses, or academic transcripts. It is virtually impossible to fake data on a blockchain, and it is highly secure, since third parties can't enter, modify, or destroy the data stored on the blockchain. So validity and security are as good as guaranteed. And to receive your documentation, you only need to wait as long as it takes to process the transaction on the blockchain, which is a matter of minutes, if not seconds, depending on the network.

Using blockchain, you could create a registry, potentially a universal registry, that can be instantly updated and pop up on your phone—without standing in line at some government office. You always have it on you (digitally), and it is instantly verifiable.

For example, say you are going to buy a bottle of vodka for a party. You are over twenty-one, but the store clerk asks for ID (good for you—you look young!). Maybe you left it at home, or you have it, but the clerk thinks it might be fake. No vodka for you. Alternatively, a blockchain ID would provide a QR code that you could bring up on your phone to be scanned and verify your age, and you don't have to go home—or to the party—empty-handed.

> **It is virtually impossible to fake data on a blockchain, and it is highly secure, since third parties can't enter, modify, or destroy the data stored on the blockchain.**

With blockchain, you can also layer information—it isn't limited to what fits on a two-by-three-inch piece of plastic. Take a vehicle title, for instance. Not only could you prove ownership of a vehicle using a blockchain-based app, but you could also pull up an individual car's history recorded on blockchain. That could include manufacturing history, number of owners, mileage, part callbacks, what repairs or upgrades have been made and when, whether the car has been involved in an accident, and other safety information. It could even send you reminders for when to change your oil or rotate your tires. All this can be recorded on blockchain and checked via a QR code scan.

Real estate is another area of concern. In Venezuela people suffered from devastating hyperinflation, millions were displaced from their country, and many lost ownership of their properties. If their records and holdings had been stored on blockchain, it would not matter where they were in the world, as they could prove whether they owned an apartment, a house, or a plot of land. You might also use smart contracts to execute wills and the inheritance of property.

Many of the current systems used to keep track of our personal data are inefficient and out of date. When I travel, I have to carry my American driver's license, my old passport, my renewed passport, my Colombian ID, and a paper copy of my Colombian visa. These are all essential documents, but they could be easily lost or stolen and be a nightmare to replace. Heck, I had a friend run his passport through the washing machine! And if I do not have the right little bit of paper, I might be denied entry into a country (or stuck in one) or blocked from conducting business. You might also think about this as it relates to rising refugee crises around the world. One of the major roadblocks to claiming asylum is that people fleeing desperate situations often do not have access to official documentation. How do you prove who you are, where you're from, and that you don't pose a threat to your potential new home country? Now imagine that there was a record of all your important personal data stored on a blockchain that you could access anywhere in the world.

Another issue with the way licenses and records are created and kept now is cost. In the United States, HIPAA compliance, which protects patient privacy, is estimated to cost $8.3 billion annually, which breaks down to each and every physician spending roughly $35,000 a year on health information technology upkeep to make sure patient records are safe and accurate.[18] That's more than some people make in a year!

Blockchain can do it more efficiently, accurately, and seamlessly. The rise of vaccine passports is proof positive of this, a number of which have been created using blockchain technology, like the International Air Transport Association (IATA) Travel Pass or OneLedger Technology's OnePass. Data can be stored securely (no central database means it's virtually impossible to hack and steal private information), and it's easy to access—all you need is a smartphone.

Voting Systems

We don't have to reach far back in history to find examples of high-stakes political dramas playing out over voting. There is of course the 2020 US presidential election, which left a majority of Republicans convinced of voter fraud.[19] Some of the main contestations were over mail-in ballots, drop boxes for paper ballots, and votes still being counted long after election day. There was no validity to their suspicion, which was largely whipped up by a button-pushing

---

18   Kim-Lien Nguyen, "HIPAA: At What Cost?" *Medical Economics*, September 9, 2019, https://www.medicaleconomics.com/view/hipaa-what-cost.

19   SRSS, "CNN Poll on Partisanship," September 12, 2021, http://cdn.cnn.com/cnn/2021/images/09/12/rel5c.-.partisanship.pdf.

right-wing media playing fast and loose with the facts, but the point is that a large number of people came away doubting the veracity of the results. Blockchain could mitigate that doubt. There was also the 2000 US presidential election between Gore and Bush that hinged on a recount of paper ballots with "hanging chads." Whatever you believe, large swathes of the population are uneasy about the integrity of the system.

Many of people's suspicions, rightly or wrongly, stem from the fact that most voting systems still use paper ballots, ticketing, and other archaic analog systems. Paper ballots are open to any number of human errors, interference, and, in rare cases, deliberate fraud. There are systems of checks and balances, ways of mitigating errors and preventing fraud, but the possibility looms large these days in the collective mind. Some voting districts or states use digital voting methods, but they are also hard to authenticate. They are susceptible to glitches and hacks, however unlikely. Another claim in the 2020 election was that voting machines were "owned" by Democrats and therefore corrupted.

Even if claims of election fraud were unproven, other countries have suffered mass voting fraud, and so we could use alternatives that protect and ensure the integrity of elections. Imagine the potential for truly free and fair elections. Would Putin still be getting 99 percent of votes?

With blockchain you can apply the same high level of authentication we have discussed with cryptocurrencies to help verify votes and voters, eliminate double counts, prevent lost or discounted votes, and create a precise record of what was voted for and when—instantaneously, with 100 percent accuracy and no middleman. It would give everyone in the country the ability to vote by verifying their voting registration with the click of a button. Not to mention, there would be no need to take off work, arrange transportation to a voting center, or wait in line for hours—some of the barriers to voting and prime reasons for low voter turnout. It would even alleviate some of the potential for voter intimidation because, well, you wouldn't even need to leave your house to do it! And because blockchain is a decentralized network, no one "owns" it in order to corrupt it.

Blockchain technology ultimately could create a more transparent, more accessible, more trustworthy system for voting.

Supply Chain Management

Supply chain management might not sound like the sexiest application of blockchain, but it could be one of the most useful and widely applied. And there are a lot of reasons we should care about supply chains. If the global pandemic taught us anything, it is that supply chains are so much more complex—and fragile—than most of us realize. It is also critically important in the face of climate change that we start paying more attention to what we consume and where it comes from. And from a business perspective, supply chain management has a huge impact on things like your bottom line and profit margins, not to mention meeting mission statements of sustainability and labor rights.

Blockchain technology can provide elegant solutions to supply chain management.

Let's take a look at how it might change the food and agriculture industries. Food and agriculture are in many ways terribly inefficient. Food gets lost or wasted at every step in the process—left to rot on the farm, lost during processing and distribution, or thrown out after it's been purchased. As much as 50 percent of food is lost before it enters the food supply.[20] In the United States, 30 to 40 percent of food—or $161 billion worth—goes to waste every year, according to the FDA.[21] And that figure more or less holds at the global level, where roughly a third of food is lost or wasted.[22] We throw out literal tons of food. There's an environmental cost to our waste, too—an estimated 8 to 10 percent of greenhouse gas emissions are associated with food that is never eaten.[23]

And there are ethical problems that plague the consumer end of food supply. How can you guarantee your food comes from where it claims to? Say you order the Alaskan salmon at a restaurant. How do you know it is truly from Alaska? Was it wild caught or scooped out of a fish farm? Was it caught legally? What were the conditions of the workers who processed it? Was the salmon treated with antibiotics or other additives? How fresh is it, or when was it caught? Such questions can't be answered accurately or honestly with current, traditional supply chain systems, which tend to be convoluted at best.

And this applies to every conceivable agricultural product.

Blockchain can solve this easily by authenticating things at every step in the supply chain. At the start of the supply chain, blockchain can provide farmers data about how much food is consumed when and by whom, which eliminates waste; it can help inform them in the decision-making process on what to grow and in what quantities

---

20 Arthur Zuckerman, "28 Food Waste Statistics 2020/2021: Causes, Impact & Solutions," Compare Camp, May 7, 2020, https://comparecamp.com/food-waste-statistics.

21 Food and Drug Administration, "Food Loss and Waste," November 19, 2021, https://www.fda.gov/food/consumers/food-loss-and-waste.

22 The World Bank, "Global Food Loss and Waste," November 22, 2021, https://datatopics.worldbank.org/what-a-waste/global_food_loss_and_waste.html.

23 United Nations Environment Programme, "UNEP Food Waste Index Report 2021," March 4, 2021, https://www.unep.org/resources/report/unep-food-waste-index-report-2021.

based on actual demand. The farmer, in exchange, can provide all of the background information on their goods—where it was produced and when and under what conditions. From there, blockchain can also smooth the process of logistics and transportation by automating processes that are currently open to human error and bureaucratic bottlenecks. There are an estimated $50 billion in losses each year to shipping and retail companies solely from mislabeled, mis-shipped, and lost or stolen cargo, meaning that someone misreads a number on a form, and there goes your inventory.[24] And if we improve efficiency in the supply chain, we can reduce waste—that includes reducing the number of trucks and freighters transporting goods and therefore reducing emissions. Smart contracts between parties will also save money for the farmer and logistics service because they eliminate the need for expensive middlemen like brokerages and lawyers. As for the retailer and then the consumer, they will know without a shadow of a doubt when, where, how, how much, and by whom something was sourced. You get not only information but also peace of mind. Push a button, scan a code—and the record is stored on blockchain, forever.

Supply chains involve enormous costs for everyone involved at every step. If you can overhaul the system with blockchain, you can save everyone money: the farmer, the distributor, the wholesaler, and the patron or consumer.

It goes without saying, this is not limited to food and agriculture. The same technology and processes can be applied to retail, energy, construction and materials, health and beauty supplies, manufacturing, pharmaceuticals, mining, electronics—we could go on all day. There is a reason that companies like FedEx, Maersk, IBM, DHL,

---

24   Sam Daley, "Making Moves: 21 Companies Using Blockchain's Logistics Capabilities to Excel," Built In, May 6, 2021, https://builtin.com/blockchain/blockchain-supply-chain-logistics-uses.

UPS, and the US Army have already adopted blockchain technology in aspects of their logistics services and supply chains.

Anticounterfeiting

Over half a billion dollars are lost each year to counterfeiting and piracy.[25] This is a huge liability, especially for luxury brands, whose goods are counterfeited all the time. China, for example, has manufacturers knocking off brands that are virtually identical to the authentic version. This causes major losses and is bad for business. If you have paid big money for something you think is going to be of a certain quality and standard, that will last for years to come, and it falls apart in the washing machine after one use, are you ever going to spend money on that brand again? And there is very little retail companies can do to stop it.

Even in cases when a brand can successfully argue in court against counterfeiters, there is very little payoff. Michael Jordan, for instance, won a landmark trademark case against a Chinese company, Qiaodan Sports Co., that was ripping off Air Jordans (and using a transliteration of "Jordan" to do so). What did he win after the protracted court battle? A whopping $46,000 in damages, a public apology, and the right to his own name.

And there is more than brand identity at stake. Counterfeited items are often associated with unethical business practices, child or slave labor, and organized crime. Part of why consumers shop for certain brands is because they believe they are supporting an ethical, sustainable business.

---

25 International Chamber of Commerce, "Counterfeiting and Piracy in 2021—The Global Impact," *World Trademark Review*, May 11, 2021, https://www.worldtrademarkreview.com/global-guide/anti-counterfeiting-and-online-brand-enforcement/2021/article/counterfeiting-and-piracy-in-2021-the-global-impact.

There are also liability issues to consider. Counterfeiting is not limited to clothing and retail goods. There are counterfeit pharmaceuticals and cosmetics, which can pose serious health risks to consumers. The World Health Organization estimates that 10 to 30 percent of drugs sold in developing countries are counterfeit.[26]

And, yet again, blockchain is the way out of this mess by providing secure, accurate authentication of goods. For example, Louis Vuitton Moët Hennessy (LVMH), a luxury conglomerate, launched their own blockchain with the help of Microsoft, called Aurora, specifically to authenticate their products—everything from the raw materials to distribution to point of sale. You can scan a QR code on the product, which instantly guarantees the product is authentic. Other luxury brands are following suit.

Here in Colombia, there are a ton of luxury knockoffs. People who want a Gucci bag often buy fake ones. Partly that is because of a dearth of luxury stores. But even still, when you go into the stores, because you are so far removed from the source, it is hard not to wonder whether the goods are real. But now you will find tags with QR cards to authenticate them. Versace shirts, for example, have tags that can be scanned to tell you if it is authenticated on Versace's own blockchain. It is genuinely helpful for the consumer trying to determine whether that shirt is, well, genuine. Not that I'm buying $300 Versace shirts, but if I wanted to, I would like to know for certain it is real.

This application of blockchain also increases the potential for secondary market sales. Traditionally, you do not see many high-end brands sold on Amazon or eBay because people cannot trust they are

---

26   International Chamber of Commerce, "5 Ways Counterfeiting Hurts Society—And What We Can Do about It," June 7, 2017, https://iccwbo.org/media-wall/news-speeches/5-ways-counterfeiting-hurts-society-and-what-we-can-do-about-it.

real—and in many cases they aren't. But if you can prove your Versace shirt is authentic, it facilitates resale. This is huge for producers and consumers alike because it increases the demand for luxury goods when consumers know there is a secondary market for buying and selling used items. You can reliably buy Louis Vuitton products online now without purchasing them directly from Louis Vuitton—and Louis Vuitton can even earn a royalty on those secondary sales (see, we're bringing it right back to the start!). And once again, there is an environmental benefit. Buying clothes and other goods secondhand extends their life cycle—keeping them out of landfills for a few more years at least.

> **Blockchain has the potential to disrupt and revitalize the way we do nearly everything.**

In the same way that some people think crypto is magical internet money, some of these blockchain solutions will sound like science fiction. But that is about as far from the truth as it gets. These are technological solutions that are already being implemented by major players across industries. Blockchain has the potential to disrupt and revitalize the way we do nearly everything—and to do it more transparently and efficiently, without waste and loss of profits, and with knock-on social and environmental benefits.

Next up, we're going to look at another moment of disruption and a unique corner of crypto: memecoins.

CHAPTER 11
MEMECOINS

I remember standing in my kitchen here in Medellín, watching CNBC in the morning, and for some reason GameStop was all over the news. I had no idea why. For those of you who don't know what GameStop is, it is the world's largest retailer of gaming systems and accessories—Xbox, PlayStation, Nintendo. And in an increasingly online world, well, their brick-and-mortar stores had become largely obsolete. I watched with rapt attention. Apparently GME, GameStop's stock, was surging in value. Inexplicably, I might add. I think most people, myself included, had no idea what was going on. It was causing a total upheaval in the market. Hedge funds were hemorrhaging billions on their balance sheets. Why was GameStop of all companies shooting to the top? A middling brick-and-mortar retail chain on the brink of bankruptcy hitting all-time highs—it made no sense.

Eventually, the driving force behind GME's meteoric rise became clear. Wall Street Bets, a group (subreddit, in the parlance) on the popular online forum Reddit, was behind the whole thing.

One of the things I love about blockchain and crypto is the inherent ethos of giving power back to the people. There is a whole vibrant community around crypto. So what I want to look at in this chapter is the internet versus Wall Street showdown of 2021 that centered around GME, AMC (movie theaters), and other stocks. On top of the drama of it all, I think it proved the point that crypto and the crypto community have a kind of collective power and influence that no one realized before then. It had been very much on the margins. But with this moment, this movement, the retail investor started fighting back in an unprecedented turn of events. And memecoins are a big part of this drama—Dogecoin, Shiba, and other memecoins that no one took seriously before. They were basically tokenized internet jokes. Unlike a lot of other cryptos, they were created for fun with no real agenda. So how did that change? What happened?

Reddit versus Robinhood

In 2020 and 2021, many folks in the United States received stimulus checks, financial subsidies, zero-interest loans, and other federal benefits connected to the pandemic. In March 2020, the stock market took a huge dive, as did crypto, but then it, like the stock market, recovered. Late in 2020, Bitcoin was starting to break out again—jumping from around $10,000 in the fall up to nearly $30,000 by the end of the year, with no sign of slowing down—and once more getting lots of media attention.[27] More people were putting money into it in hopes of getting rich or at least making enough to get out of the system. It seemed like a good hedge against all the normal investing routes that were crashing amid the disruption of the pandemic.

So, meanwhile, certain hedge funds were trying to short certain publicly traded companies. The best known was GameStop. GameStop

---

[27] Coin Market Cap, "Bitcoin Historical Data," November 24, 2021, https://coinmarket-cap.com/currencies/bitcoin/historical-data/.

was suffering during the pandemic. They were losing revenue because their stores were closed due to COVID-19 restrictions and lockdowns. And hedge funds did what hedge funds do: they saw an opportunity to short GME and crush the stock to make massive profits.

Here is a primer for readers who do not know how shorting works: Imagine you want to sell an apple because you think the price of apples is going to go down. Say one apple is worth ten dollars, but you expect it to dip to five next month. But you don't actually own any apples. However, if someone loaned you an apple, with interest, you could sell it for ten bucks today, wait till its value declines, then buy that apple back at five dollars, returning the apple to the lender (plus interest) while walking away with a tidy five-dollar profit.

This is done on the stock market at large scale with companies all the time. Short sellers can leverage a position, borrow stock from a company, sell it in order to buy it back at a lower price, and make gobs of money, basically out of thin air. Obviously for this plan to succeed, the price of stock (or apples) has to actually go down. If the apple goes up in price instead of down, you would be on the hook to pay more than your ten dollars for the apple in order to pay back the lender. And the price could theoretically go up and up and up with no limit.

So hedge funds were aggressively borrowing GME stock, selling it, then lending it to their buddies who would then sell it, then those guys would lend it to other players who would sell it again—all in order to crash the stock price, close out the short sale by buying it back, and make bank. What they did not anticipate was that GME would go *up* in price. And that is exactly what happened. It started to skyrocket. That meant that the hedge funds had to shell out billions to buy back GME at a much higher price.

What triggered the rise in price was primarily Reddit's /r/wallstreetbets (WSB), a group of internet-dwelling amateur investors. The group makes calls on the market they think will benefit retail investors. One Redditor, u/deepfuckingvalue (later revealed to be Keith Gill), posted that a hedge fund was trying to short GME, so WSB banded together to counter this move. WSB at the time had over 2.5 million members; some were small investors, others with deeper pockets. Everyone piled in to buy GME, and it started surging in price, reaching record highs, achieving staggering numbers and gains you would usually only see in cryptos. To give you an idea of just how successful, Gill reported $34 million in returns, nearly $20 million in total gains, from GME.[28] (Other sources cite this as up to $48 million in returns.)[29]

The swift rise caught hedge funds and Wall Street in general off guard, and it forced the hedge funds to buy back into GME just to recover their position, which of course pushed GME stock even higher in price. So there was this crazy snowball effect. Ultimately, it sent GameStop, a struggling company, into Fortune 500 territory.

When I say this was unprecedented, I mean there was literally no precedent for something like this happening. None. And it didn't stop there. The WSB group, buoyed by their success, became a subculture unto itself, a David versus Goliath struggle where ordinary people and retail investors could fight back against a crooked, corrupt financial system.

---

28 u/deepfuckingvalue, "GME YOLO Update—Apr 16 2021—Final Update," r/wallstreetbets, Reddit, https://www.reddit.com/r/wallstreetbets/comments/msblc3/gme_yolo_update_apr_16_2021_final_update.

29 Jason Daughty, "Meet u/deepfuckingvalue, the GameStop Investor Upending Wall Street," The Entrepreneur Fund, January 30, 2021, https://theentrepreneurfund.com/meet-u-deepfuckingvalue-the-gamestop-investor-upending-wall-street.

Next they began to pile into other companies they traditionally liked, or companies that were struggling, more or less as a joke—frankly, these were companies that these Redditors probably identified with. The WSB culture is pretty self-deprecating; they refer to themselves as apes. They've got a real sense of humor and self-awareness, and in this case, a strong sense of solidarity. If they all hung in there together, they could stick it to the system, have a bit of a laugh, and maybe even make some decent money. So next they bought up AMC Entertainment stock just because people liked movies. Then they piled investments into BlackBerry, pretty much a dead company because, well, who has a BlackBerry these days? And that, too, skyrocketed. Nokia came next and shot up in price. Like dominos, they went one after the other, basically as a joke, but one that had a very real impact on the market and these companies. People started referring to these as meme stocks, stocks that see a surge in viral activity, usually through social media platforms like Reddit and Twitter.

Many of these small investors were using Robinhood, a simple phone app for trading stocks that is popular with younger investors. Robinhood saw that its platform was being used for this meme stock frenzy and put a stop to it. Seeing the irony in a company called Robinhood trying to quash the little guy, *BuzzFeed* reported on this as, "People Are Accusing Robinhood of Stealing from the Poor to Give to the Rich after It Limited Trading on GameStop Shares," and they weren't wrong.[30] And, in contrast, a lot of the WSB investors were using their stock market earnings to do good things in their communities. For example, a bunch of them used their GME money

---

30   Clarissa-Jan Lim, "People Are Accusing Robinhood of Stealing from the Poor to Give to the Rich after It Limited Trading on GameStop Shares," *BuzzFeed*, January 28, 2021, https://www.buzzfeednews.com/article/clarissajanlim/robinhood-gamestop-amc-stock-twitter-wall-street.

to buy Nintendo Switches and other gear from GameStop to donate to children's hospitals.[31]

The other major player in this story was Citadel Securities, a trading firm and so-called market maker because they get to see what stocks people are buying and selling in real time. Robinhood makes money by selling financial data to companies including and like Citadel. Citadel leveraged its massive influence over Robinhood and basically strong-armed them into blocking purchases of these meme stocks to protect the hedge funds' interest. This infuriated people and highlighted how much market manipulation exists despite claims of being a fair and even playing field. It made it abundantly clear that the elites would bend the rules to halt retail trading to protect their own interests. This only galvanized the WSB community and others who were tired of being screwed over by the system. And as the story broke on mainstream media, the outrage bled into the mainstream, too.

There was a proposed class action lawsuit against Robinhood and Citadel for collusion. Keith Gill was among the investors called to testify in front of Congress. But the suit was eventually dismissed in November 2021.

---

31 Hannah Jones, "North Texas Investor Uses GameStop Gains to Help Sick Children," *NCB Dallas Fort Worth*, January 29, 2021, https://www.nbcdfw.com/news/national-international/north-texas-investor-uses-gamestop-gains-help-sick-children/2537134/; u/cockinaclock, "GameStop Gear Going to the New Home at the Children's Hospital of Atlanta Monday. POWER TO THE PLAYERS!" r/wallstreetbets, Reddit, March 2021, https://www.reddit.com/r/wallstreetbets/comments/mf0msr/gamestop_gear_going_to_the_new_home_at_the; u/Lunar033, "I am Proud to Do My Part in Paying Forward Our Good Fortune with a Donation of 6 Nintendo Switches and Games to Go with Them to the Children's Minnesota Hospital. Can't Stop. Won't Stop. GameStop. (Still Long 50 Shares I WILL NOT SELL)," r/wallstreetbets, Reddit, February 2021, https://www.reddit.com/r/wallstreetbets/comments/l90oq6/i_am_proud_to_do_my_part_in_paying_forward_our.

The Rise of Memecoins

What does this have to do with crypto, you ask? Having been essentially forced off the playing field, the Wall Street Bets subculture then cast its eye outside the traditional markets to continue waging war against the system (while making money for its members). So they started gravitating toward crypto. What better place could they go to pump an asset and send a giant *eff you* to the system?

So lots of capital moved from the stock market into crypto. But the apes were not buying the large-cap tokens like bitcoin and ether. True to form, they went after the one thing that has no real purpose, was started as a joke, has no real history or anything fundamental to back its value or to suggest it would be useful in the future: Dogecoin (DOGE). There really is nothing that special about it. I have been in the space a long time, and DOGE has nothing going for it except that it has been around for a while. But everyone piled into DOGE, and like all their other investments, the price shot upward. In a sense, DOGE's greatest use case is as a means of voicing protest with your money against the manipulated, Wall Street-dominated markets.

By now this internet subculture was catching the attention of lots of folks, including billionaires. In particular, Elon Musk, who is vocal on social media and has a big following, put in his two cents on DOGE. Actually, he put in a lot more than two cents. He started touting DOGE publicly and posting DOGE memes. He became its richest and most influential cheerleader. This helped to legitimize DOGE as a real asset.

In late January and early February 2021, it started to shoot up in value.[32] One day it was up 330 percent, another 200 percent the next day. By February, it had grown by 956.9 percent. In April, it started

---

32 Coin Market Cap, "Dogecoin Historical Data," November 24, 2011, https://coinmarketcap.com/currencies/dogecoin/historical-data/.

to hit double digits (still on the right side of the decimal, but still!). So from January 1 to May 8, it went from $0.004 to $0.737. Since the start of the year, it is incredibly still up nearly 5,000 percent (as of this writing at the end of 2021), even after falling from its all-time high.

Mark Cuban is another public advocate of Dogecoin; he allows the Dallas Mavericks to accept it as payment. AMC theaters, ironically, also now allows it. Some crypto platforms and exchanges have listed DOGE and allow it to be traded, further mainstreaming it.

It just goes to show how powerful this community can be. And all the publicity and excitement around DOGE's rise served to garner more interest and support in crypto from the little guy eager to escape the drudgery of the financial system. Dogecoin thus became a subculture itself and sparked demand for different obscure assets that retail investors can pump up through online communities. The idea is that an ordinary person can multiply their money via memecoins many times over, all while giving the system a taste of its own medicine.

That said, it is extremely volatile and risky because these coins tend to fall as rapidly as they rise.

Shiba Inu (SHIB) may be even more popular than Dogecoin. Its followers are trying to do the same thing as DOGE but on a bigger level. It was created alongside DOGE, and people are speculating that it will keep going up tremendously in value.

There was a story that broke in the news recently about SHIB.[33] A man invested $8,000 in SHIB one year ago when it was worth nothing. Today, his investment is worth $5.7 billion. Billion with a *b*. It is absurd. Unreal. That is the result of Shiba Inu spiking 103 *million* percent. It's mind-boggling.

---

33 Matthew Fox, "A Crypto Wallet Shows an Investor Made an $8,000 Shiba Inu Coin Purchase Last Year. Today, It Is Worth $5.7 Billion," *Business Insider*, October 28, 2021, https://markets.businessinsider.com/news/currencies/crypto-investor-turned-8000-into-5-billion-buying-shiba-inu-2021-10.

And it is all part of this new subculture. A subculture that is emerging, shifting, nebulous, and hard to even name. But it coalesces around DOGE, SHIBA, and other lesser known memecoins like Baby Doge Coin, Santa Inu, or SHARIK TOKEN. And it is the direct descendent of the GME craze of 2021.

The Future of Memecoins

On some level these coins are a pump and dump: The price goes up, savvy investors cash out, and the price crashes. But there is a legitimate market around them, and if you know how to trade, you can do well and make a profit. Memecoins are highly susceptible to the same kind of crowd psychology that operates in other areas of the financial markets.

Memecoins are a new niche in blockchain. We have talked about DeFi, dapps, stablecoins, CBDCs, and other things, but memecoins are something unto themselves. They started as a joke, but they are real and probably here to stay. Again, they are highly volatile, but the potential reward corresponds to its high risk. It is truly a novel phenomenon and a bellwether of the age. If nothing else, memecoins also generate a lot of interest in crypto in general and provide an entrée into the space, particularly since they tend to be buoyed by very active, supportive communities.

I doubt DOGE will solve real-world problems or make life better for the masses the way other crypto and blockchain applications will. But it does serve as a voice to repudiate the centralized financial system, Wall Street, and the big players.

For my part, I have invested small amounts in these coins for fun, and at times I've even made a little bit (other times I've made nothing). I largely did it to get on board and be part of that community, feel a part of a *movement* that is really challenging the powers that be.

Beyond the pump and dump dynamics, the community's ethos is one I agree with: to take power back and give people a better, fairer, more transparent system. I am not in it to make a killing on any of these. I just want to participate in the movement. And truthfully, I think that's how a lot of people inside the community feel, too.

I know some people who have made a fortune from memecoins as well as people who have gone in heavy near the top and lost quite a lot of money. I can't in good faith recommend investing in something so volatile if you don't know what you're doing and don't know how to manage risk. The high risk, high reward is not for the faint of heart or shallow of pocket.

Memecoins, even DOGE and SHIB, do not have a long market history. That means you can't analyze it the same way you can for bitcoin. I can look at a thousand charts for bitcoin, analyze the data down to the last iota of information, and evaluate whether it is a good investment. Memecoins don't have that history. That is part of the reason that larger investors and institutions still don't take memecoins seriously. They are in many ways the opposite of what established investors would traditionally buy, especially because the memecoins are largely motivated by resentment to institutional players, hedge funds, and so-called whales. (Dogecoin is the weird exception to this rule, having been somewhat legitimized despite the fact it has no fundamental value, unless you count popular support.)

But they do offer clues about market psychology. You can look at a chart for DOGE and infer whether there are rumblings of greed or fear and try to predict where the price is going next. You can also measure how people have moved money from DOGE to SHIB and to other memecoins, then look at trade volume and correlate that with level of interest via the internet (e.g., volume of tweets or Google Trends). You can also look at indicators like an increase of memes around shibacoin or the number of Shiba Inu wallet addresses. Using these metrics, you can make a strong, or at least more informed, guess around market psychology and probably make a good trade. It is a different skill, one in which Bollinger Bands, stochastics, and other conventional trading metrics do not do much good. Memecoins are rife with opportunity if you know how to read the writing on the wall.

There are not many memecoins beyond Dogecoin and Shiba Inu that have had much success or headline coverage. But I guarantee by the time this book comes out there will be another one. There are plenty out there competing to be the next big thing. What the market shifts to next is anyone's guess. It's a wild ride that we are all on together, and we don't know what is around the bend, but something is coming.

Meanwhile, the conversation around the GameStop debacle is likely to continue—particularly as more retail investors get involved in the space—and I hope it does. Dialogue is good. The system is rotten; it needs to change. And now retail investors are feeling their power. The culture is there, and it is only going to keep growing. I think it is a dynamic, interesting niche within blockchain that will be around for a long time to come.

> **Memecoins are rife with opportunity if you know how to read the writing on the wall.**

We have talked a lot about the crypto community, not just in relation to memecoins but throughout the world of blockchain. So how can you get involved? What does that look like? Next we'll dive a little deeper into how you might launch your own dapp or develop a new blockchain application. There are pretty much endless possibilities, so gear up and get in!

CHAPTER 12
PICK YOUR PLATFORM

We have looked at blockchain inside and out and explored some of the most promising real-world applications for it. Now we are going to discover what it is like to get involved in another big part of the crypto community: development. What does it look like to work in the blockchain space? There is one particularly important question we have yet to answer if you want to build your own blockchain application: What platform should you build your applications on? So in this chapter, we are going to look at that question from a virtual perspective, evaluating which digital platform will serve developers and business owners best.

First of all, a platform is something that you build on blockchain. Think of it like building a website on the internet. There are a lot of things built on blockchain such as databases, platforms, engines, or generators, depending on what the use case for the application is going to be. Again using the internet as a parallel, Facebook is a platform, Google is a database, and those run on the network of the internet. For blockchain, an example might

> **A platform is something that you build on blockchain.**

151

be that Ethereum is the blockchain, and OpenSea is the platform. To understand this better, let's look at some of the most innovative existing platforms and their use cases.

Filecoin and Digital Storage

We touched on Filecoin briefly in chapter 5, but now I want to look at it from the angle of a developer rather than an investor. Filecoin developed the InterPlanetary File System (IPFS), its native blockchain, which more or less enables you to create a whole new Web 3.0 for the internet, including websites, landing pages, and search engines. Its network encompasses everything done online now but in a decentralized fashion.

There is a whole network built on the Filecoin platform. It has a unique use case and one I personally like a lot: decentralized storage. It is similar to cloud storage services like Google Drive or Dropbox, except it works over decentralized networks. This means it is cheaper, more secure (no central point of failure or access point), and anyone can make money in the network. To do that, you can offer extra storage by connecting it to Filecoin's network and getting paid in filecoin. It is a closed-loop system that is effective and growing, and it solves some issues that exist in traditional corporate cloud storage providers.

I expect some of the big cloud providers to use something like the Filecoin network, which would save companies and users money. The decentralized model is simply faster, cheaper, and better. For creators, developers, and businesses, it offers a ton of possibilities.

Solana and the Future of Gaming

This blockchain is very popular because of how scalable it is. Many networks are building various platforms on Solana. It is especially popular in the gaming space. Many video game companies are building platforms for gaming that can be played in virtual reality or the metaverse. One example is a game called *Star Atlas*, which is a giant intergalactic metaverse; it is a game but also a platform unto itself. *Star Atlas* is an open world where you can travel, explore, collect items, battle opponents—basically, everything cool you do in a video game. You can also create non-fungible tokens for in-game items, like an upgraded spaceship, stylish clothes for your avatar, or an advanced weapon. And it is all run on Solana's blockchain.

For creators, developers, and businesses, it offers a ton of possibilities.

You can create value in what you do in the game that can even be transferred to another game. Consider *Halo*, a hugely successful first-person shooter video game that utilizes an open world concept. Imagine if *Halo* as a gaming platform allowed you to take what you had in one *Halo* version and use it in another. For example, the pistol in *Halo 1* is notoriously way overpowered. Imagine creating an NFT of that pistol and taking it into *Halo 2*, *3*, or *4* and using it there or selling it to another player.

So *Star Atlas* is creating a marketplace, an in-world economy within a gaming ecosystem, that in my estimation is likely to expand and grow more complex given that millions of people are online gaming every day. It's a huge untapped reservoir. *Star Atlas* will be one of the first mega-games but also a platform within the game. It is truly revolutionary and exciting.

Cosmos and the Universe of Blockchain Apps

Cosmos has kind of a different approach. What distinguishes Cosmos is they seek to create an interconnected economy across blockchains and platforms, or the internet of blockchains, as they like to say. The basic model is a bunch of different blockchains, which they call zones, that meet at a central blockchain, referred to as a hub. And in building their network this way, they have created apps and platforms that are interconnected and can interact. It is very scalable and fast, qualities that every new generation of blockchain desires.

There are a lot of use cases for a model like this. So far, they have created crypto wallets, VPNs, and databases, among other applications. Exodus, whose CEO, JP Richardson, appeared on *BlockHash*, is one of the many apps using Cosmos. It has an entire platform within its wallet that lets you buy, sell, and trade assets. They also plan to enable users to seek leverage, obtain loans, and invest directly in the company. There is also Sentinel dVPN, a decentralized VPN. It is cheaper than most traditional or centralized VPNs. Because it runs on decentralized nodes, it's also more private, which is the whole purpose behind VPNs. There are definitely centralized VPNs that log your activity, and they aren't always particularly candid about doing so. ShapeShift, a popular trading platform, uses Cosmos, as do many other crypto exchanges. So, as you can see, it is a highly popular platform for a wide variety of apps because it synchronizes currently atomized platforms.

The goal of Cosmos is interconnectedness: letting people do more in one single place instead of using different platforms. And if the idea of interconnectedness doesn't make sense, let's compare Cosmos to Ethereum to help clarify what it means. Ethereum is a blockchain that lets you create applications and platforms, but those apps and platforms don't really share an ecosystem or share services, even if they have the same origin. You build CryptoKitties on Ethereum, and you build CryptoPunks on Ethereum; they are both NFT collections, but they are not necessarily connected to each other in any concrete way.

The whole goal of Cosmos is to create an internet of blockchains in an ever-expanding ecosystem where all these apps, services, platforms, exchanges, and anything you build on it are gathered under one digital roof.

Tezos and NFTs

So let's pick up with that last example of NFTs. We have talked a lot about NFTs—the whole of chapter 6 was dedicated to them—but we have done so primarily in connection with Ethereum. But as NFTs evolve, they will need more advanced platforms, maybe even a more evolved blockchain. That could be Ethereum 2.0, but more likely the solution will be the development of NFTs on other blockchains as well.

One in particular will likely be Tezos. Its blockchain can constantly evolve and amend itself without having to rely on consensus or forking the blockchain to make a major change. It is more flexible in that regard, making it an attractive place for developers. Lately, it has provided an especially appealing platform for folks who are building NFTs. It also happens to be, as of now at least, a little cheaper and more energy efficient than Ethereum.

Tezos offers a big variety of tools to build NFTs, which empowers creators to experiment and innovate more than they can on, say, Ethereum. Ethereum, in contrast, has restrictions on which tokens can be used, making it hard to batch large numbers of NFTs without big transaction fees.

As I write this, the Art Basel fair is taking place in Miami Beach. It is a big deal in the art world, and NFT artists are joining in and getting a lot of attention. Many of those artists are building on Tezos rather than on Ethereum, drawn by its variety of tools and lower fees that let them mint and distribute their artwork. So Tezos is making a big splash in Art Basel. I would expect Tezos to remain a strong competitor to Ethereum, especially in the NFT and platform creation space.

OpenBazaar and the Blockchain-Based Marketplace

OpenBazaar is not as popular as it once was, but it remains an important platform. It has been around for a long time; in fact, it is one of the earliest platform use cases to run on blockchain. Its prototype or beta version, DarkMarket, actually started as a proof of concept project in response to the shutdown of Silk Road.

OpenBazaar is kind of like a decentralized Amazon (and we all know we need a viable alternative to the monolith that is Amazon). It is a marketplace, and on the marketplace you can buy and sell basically anything you want—that includes digital and physical items. And you can conduct business across borders. They even sell short-term rentals, like Airbnb but without the annoying, costly fees. It is an open-source software, so there are no fees to use the platform or make trades. That also means it cannot be censored, is restriction-free, and lets users transact semi-anonymously.

It is reputation and ratings-based, just like eBay or Amazon. That said, implementing a ratings and reputation system in a decentralized space has been difficult. Obviously, relying on the reputation of anonymous decentralized sellers involves risk. So on OpenBazaar, if a seller fails to respond to a customer's inquiry, fails to deliver a product, or does anything else that would warrant alarm, their reputation score would be dented. Likewise for customers: If you don't pay a seller or otherwise act as a nuisance, you'll lose reputation points. It isn't a perfect system, but there are some checks and balances in place.

Originally OpenBazaar only used bitcoin for buying and selling on the platform, but it has since expanded to include bitcoin cash, litecoin, and Zcash and plans to expand to accept even more tokens in the future.

I suspect that regardless of whether OpenBazaar succeeds or fails in the future, as one of the pioneers, it will have paved the way for similar decentralized marketplaces. Who knows? Maybe it will become a staunch competitor of Amazon itself one day.

Hello Pal and Social Media

Hello Pal is a social media platform for global chat and livestreaming. It has built-in translation technology because the app is geared toward travel and language learning. That also means it is aimed at a global market. Using the app, you can go live from your phone and interact directly with your audience.

The platform leverages blockchain technology to help creators make money and reward their audience. The platform has its own token, palto (PLT), but also uses bitcoin and ether. Say you start a livestream, and someone likes it; they can reward you in tokens, or you can request tokens for users to access the stream. It gives creators new ways to monetize their content. You can even reward listeners and viewers with unique tokens to create incentives.

Unlike creators on traditional social media platforms, Hello Pal creators don't have to court third parties for ads and promotions. I might have millions of followers on Instagram, but it is difficult to make money on that following unless I have some kind of influencer sponsorship or corporate partnership. Not to mention that traditional social media markets are being flooded with content, which can push creators out into smaller and smaller margins. I mean, how many yoga models do you need pushing Lululemon on Instagram?

Platform Playground

So, as you can see, it is not as easy as saying: If you want to build a blockchain-based app, use such and such platform. Different platforms offer different benefits for different use cases. You have to consider what your use case is going to be, the scalability of the platform, the adoption rate (how big the user base and projected growth are), the variety of tools available to a developer, other unique features of the platform, and how easy it is to work with a particular platform's blockchain in relation to your own experience as a developer. There is a lot to consider.

And it is worth noting again just how much more blockchain has to offer beyond making fast cash in bitcoin and that we are still very much in the early development for a lot of these new platforms and associated apps. It is very much open to new developers, investors, and businesses who want to get involved. The ship has definitely not left the harbor. The ship is actually still being built.

In the next chapter, we will examine another of the practicalities of working on blockchain—virtual place. Next up: physical place. What are the hot spots geographically for working in the blockchain space?

CHAPTER 13
LOCATION, LOCATION, LOCATION

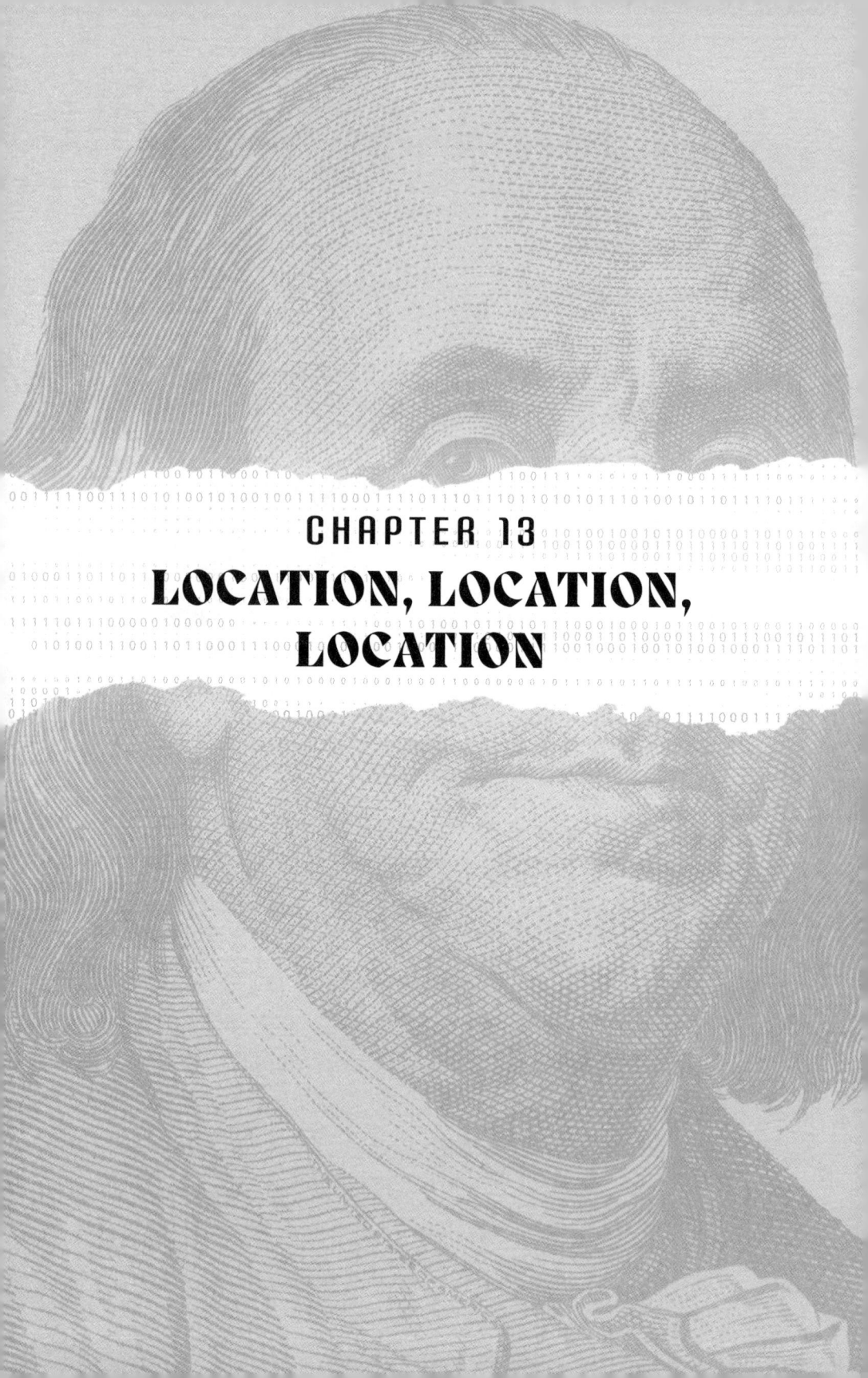

Now through to the end of the book, we are going to focus exclusively on what it's like to work in the field. A big part of working in crypto is the lifestyle and the opportunities that open up for you once you join the industry. So what are the places worldwide where blockchain is booming? How might your choice of location affect your life and work in the industry? Obviously, one of the major advantages of working in a digital field is you can work from almost anywhere in the world as long as you have good Wi-Fi.

I grew up in Oregon, went to college in Los Angeles, spent time in Las Vegas, and traveled all over the United States. The US has a lot to offer, but in

> A big part of working in crypto is the lifestyle and the opportunities that open up for you once you join the industry.

many ways, to me it seems stuck in its ways. It is increasingly politically divided and rancorous. Not to mention, the cost of living is high; the dollar is being inflated. And it is a difficult place to bootstrap a business. Because of issues like access to capital, regulations, taxes, and licensing—which often conflict between state and federal requirements—the US ranked 51 out of 190 countries for ease of starting a business in the World Bank's annual report.[34] It can be a stifling environment for business, innovation, and comfortable living—with a handful of notable exceptions.

After traveling extensively and getting a feel for different places, I decided to base myself in Medellín, Colombia. I wanted to put down roots in a place with more opportunity in this field. What I like about Colombia is that it is developing and growing quickly, trending up, evolving from one of the most dangerous places in the world to one of the safest, and is still early in its growth curve. By the end of the decade, Medellín could very well be the next Miami. Development is not slowing down, and money is flowing in. Business-wise, it makes sense. In crypto, the market is less saturated than other places, but demand is high.

And I just love the people, the weather (it's called the City of Eternal Spring), the food, and the nearby cities and towns in Colombia. I never get bored here, and there is always something new to experience. It is an ideal place for young people with dreams and a flair for living well. Medellín has a bright future, and Colombia as a country is moving in the right direction. For the meantime, I don't plan on going anywhere.

So if you want to work for a particular company or industry, or you just want to be plugged into the community around you, there are some standout cities for blockchain. I visited many of these places on my search for where I ultimately wanted to land. Here are some of the best places to set up shop in the crypto community.

---

34 Leigh Buchanan, "Here's Why It's So Hard to Start a Business in the US," *Inc.*, October 26, 2016, https://www.inc.com/leigh-buchanan/why-its-so-hard-to-start-a-business-in-the-us.html.

Vancouver, Canada

The first time I visited Vancouver was in 2015 for the Sprott Stansberry Conference, which has since been rebranded as the Sprott Natural Resource Symposium. It is a three-day affair all about precious metals, mining, investment opportunities, small-cap stocks, and the like. We would sit in a room with boomers and learn about an industry no one is actually interested in, but it can be profitable if you invest prudently. Hence why I went every summer—before I got into crypto, that is. But around this same time, Bitcoin had its first big runup before the 2017 mega-rally.

Vancouver is a gorgeous city. It has earned the nickname of the Emerald City for the green sheen of its glassy buildings and bay vistas. It has most things you want in a city: good food, interesting people, cool weather in the summer. I have always enjoyed visiting. And a fun bit of trivia: Vancouver is home to the world's first bitcoin ATM. When I was there, I visited one of their big malls where I saw a bitcoin ATM, probably the first one I had ever seen. And there was a *line* to use it! It was a novelty. People wanted to buy some bitcoin and try it out. It's great to see it as part of everyday life. So there is a definite start-up/tech culture. And crypto has found a home there, too.

One reason is that today the province is regulation-friendly and encourages people to start blockchain-related projects. Cryptocurrencies are not considered legal tender in Canada, but they can be used to pay for goods and services at shops and online stores that accept them; Vancouver boasts over one hundred stores that accept crypto as payment.[35] Crypto exchanges (like Binance and Coinbase) are regulated in the same ways as normal money service businesses, and regular tax laws apply to crypto transactions, which seems to be

---

35   Marija Pandurov, "11+ Cryptic Cryptocurrency Canada Statistics for 2021," *ReviewLution*, https://reviewlution.ca/resources/cryptocurrency-canada-statistics.

the way most countries are going. Canada also ranks sixth globally for number of running bitcoin nodes (although the number one spot belongs to Satoshi, so Canada is really fifth when it comes to country rankings).[36]

Vancouver also attracts a lot of Asian tourists, especially Chinese and Koreans. So technologically and financially, they tend to have the same technology as China, often before it arrives in the United States. It's common for people in Vancouver to pay for purchases with WeChat and Alipay. At the time I was there, American credit cards did not even have the electronic chip. I remember sitting down for lunch and how surprised I was to see this new technology out of Asia where you just pop in the card, it reads your chip, and the purchase is transacted. So Vancouver is a tech-forward city with a history of cashless banking and commerce.

Today, there are tons of job opportunities in the crypto space, and the city offers a great quality of life.

Panama City, Panama

I visited Panama City in 2018. It's off the radar for most people, but there is an insane amount of wealth there in large part because of the Panama Canal. It also means the city has a legacy of foreign investment and international trade. They have renovated the airport and seem to be on a skyscraper building boom. The city offers great shopping and a remarkable diversity of people. It bridges North and South America, so a lot of money and people flow through, and into, Panama. It is a desirable place to live, with its easy living conditions and great weather. And it's a direct flight away from most cities in the United States.

---

36   Bitnodes, "Global Bitcoin Nodes Distribution," December 7, 2021, https://bitnodes.io.

When I was there, I visited a colonial town, Casco Viejo, that was founded in the 1600s (in case the name didn't give it away, it means "old town"). It is a popular tourist spot. At night the bars and clubs on the rooftops come alive. It's a vibrant place to eat and drink and go dancing. One night I was out and about and was surprised to find that many of the bars accepted payment in bitcoin, and that was back in 2018. Credit and debit cards were not widely accepted there, but bitcoin was. It was a lucky turn of events for me because I didn't have any cash on me, so I ended up paying for drinks in bitcoin.

Today Panama is tech-friendly and open to crypto and blockchain. Panama is currently trying to pass a bill to make bitcoin legal tender in the country. This would mean residents could pay bills and taxes in bitcoin, without exception, and merchants nationwide would accept it. It also has a big advantage to start-ups. Because taxes are only levied on income earned in-country, digital businesses that earn profits outside of Panama effectively don't pay tax.[37] So if you want to launch your crypto empire from a place with a middle-income country lifestyle but low-income country expenses, Panama might be right for you.

Buenos Aires, Argentina

That same year, I visited Argentina. The people there were struggling. The Argentine peso had crashed, and the country was in a monetary crisis (again, as a result of high inflation). A lot of middle-class people lost their savings, and the government was doing little to support its citizens. I could have a *choripán*, a salad, and a beer for around $2 USD because the peso was so devalued. Even an upscale lunch at

---

37   Dean Steinback, "Will Panama Be the Next Top Crypto Jurisdiction?" *Crypto Law Insider,* October 26, 2018, https://cryptolawinsider.com/panama.

the exclusive Four Seasons Hotel only cost about $15, inclusive of drinks. I remember exchanging $100 USD for pesos and getting a huge stack of pesos—I had to hide it in my coat—it was a real symbol of inflation.

I learned a lot while I was there about how the economy was being hammered by IMF loans. A lot of businesses did not even want to accept pesos because they were worth so little. I ended up paying for a lot of things in USD or bitcoin. People preferred bitcoin over their own currency. They were trying to find a way out of the fiat money system, building something new out of necessity in the midst of a crisis. In a tanking economy, Bitcoin offered some hope, or at least an alternative.

Today, inflation is still rife, and they are still in an ongoing economic downturn. As such, there is a huge demand among the public for bitcoin and crypto, and lots of people are signing up to crypto exchanges. Buenos Aires is also a hot spot for crypto mining because the cost of electricity is so low. A recent report ranked Argentina as twenty-first in the world in realized bitcoin gains last year.[38] President Alberto Fernández has signaled that his government is open to the idea of adopting crypto as legal tender, which is promising for the industry as a whole. If you're in the crypto space, Argentina is another possible base for developing a career or launching a blockchain project.

---

38   Agustino Fontevecchia, "A Crypto-Revolution in Argentina," *Forbes*, June 28, 2021, https://www.forbes.com/sites/afontevecchia/2021/06/28/a-crypto-revolution-in-argentina.

Medellín, Colombia

I am a little biased on this one. Most of my crypto experience has taken place here in Colombia. I had visited the country several times, and eventually I decided to move here. So I have seen the way the city has grown with crypto. Around 2019, as I got to know more people, I began seeing more people using and talking about it.

That year some friends visited me in Medellín. We wanted to go to this small city on a lake, called Guatapé—a sunny, picturesque town with great food and lots of activities for tourists. My friends and I hopped on a bus to hike up the stone monolith that is the symbol of Guatapé called La Piedra ("the Rock"). We did not bring any cash because we were so used to using credit cards in Medellín. Even in a small town, we figured most merchants would still accept credit cards. But Guatapé was different. So after our hike, we were pretty hungry, as you might imagine. We wanted to get lunch in town but realized no one accepted cards anywhere, and we could not find an ATM. So not only could we not buy a meal, but we also hadn't bought our return tickets to Medellín. What could we do? We were getting a little desperate, actually: strange town, no money, no way to pay for anything, and no ride back. Oh—and the kicker—one of my friends lost her wallet while we were there.

Finally, we found one restaurant whose chalkboard outside read, "We accept bitcoin!" We went in and ordered four beers, four arepas, and some pesos so we could buy a bus ticket back. We paid for everything in bitcoin, relaxed for a bit, and then boarded the last bus home. So that day bitcoin actually saved my ass.

Now there are bitcoin ATMs all over Medellín, and there is a vibrant software culture. The city is striving to be a Latin Silicon Valley and encouraging start-ups and tech investment. And Medellín is also a fantastic place to live. It is laid back and friendly; people here know how to live life. It is especially great if you are young and want to start somewhere fresh.

I have started a company here, Blocolombia, and I relocated my consulting business from the US to Medellín. We are building out our client list, which now includes Colombian notables like Senator Juan Felipe Lemos Uribe. He is aiming to be the "Blockchain Senator" and is working with us closely to bring the technology to Colombia.

Medellín is very open to embracing new technologies, especially blockchain. Some forward-thinking politicians are trying to pass legislation involving blockchain voting, notaries, and registration. The big banks have partnerships with Gemini, Binance, and other major cryptocurrency exchanges. It is definitely emerging as a vital crypto hub. Sure, I'm partial to the city because I love living here, but anyone who is young and ambitious and creative would thrive in Medellín.

Miami, Florida

Miami may not seem super exotic (unless maybe you're reading this in Minnesota), but it is firmly on the crypto map. Miami is trying to position itself as a crypto city. This drive gained momentum during the pandemic as a way to attract new business to a city hard hit by the lockdown. Miami has been actively courting blockchain companies and innovators.

The mayor, Francis Suarez, a smart young guy, is leading the charge to make Miami a crypto capital. He made headlines after taking his paycheck in bitcoin. He has been quoted as saying he wants to "make sure that no city or state has more favorable laws and regulations" than Miami.[39] Now he is touting a Miami-specific crypto called

---

39 Rachel McIntosh, "Wanna Start a Crypto Business? Consider Miami, Says Mayor Francis Suarez," *Finance Magnates*, February 8, 2021, https://www.financemagnates.com/cryptocurrency/news/wanna-start-a-crypto-business-consider-miami-says-mayor-francis-suarez.

MiamiCoin, which lets people invest in the city and serves as a form of payment; digital wallets are already being set up for Miami residents.

Some of the biggest crypto conventions take place in Miami, like the CryptoWorldCon International Blockchain and Crypto Conference, Bitcoin 2022, and Miami Crypto World. Miami is also a hub for NFT development and exploration, bolstered by its reputation as a longtime center for athletes and artists. So it's an ideal place for networking. Miami is a very wealthy city, so there's a lot of potential investment capital to flow into blockchain.

Many stores and businesses accept not just bitcoin but also dogecoin, ether, and litecoin. It's an explorative, progressive city eager to embrace the future. There are signs around the city that say, "Bitcoin accepted here" and billboards that read, "Fuck the banks." Again, this is another big mission of the mayor, to get bitcoin accepted everywhere in the city.

The downside is that Miami is expensive; living costs are high. But to open a business in an international metropolis with well-heeled clients and investors offers its own kind of advantage. For the time being, Miami is *the* place to be if you have money and want to invest or participate in crypto.

New York, Austin, and Dallas are trying to follow in Miami's footsteps, but for now, Miami is still the place for crypto in the US.

Before we move away from the western hemisphere, it's worth talking about Silicon Valley and San Francisco, which are the traditional tech hubs in the US. Are they lagging behind when it comes to crypto? Yes and no. Obviously some of the biggest tech companies and innovators are located in Silicon Valley, and in general it is a crypto-friendly place. Coinbase, for example, was founded in San Francisco. Traditional centers of software and technology are promoting crypto, but the rate of growth is much higher in other cities than in the traditional centers of technology and finance. The same is true of London, Paris, New York, and Shenzhen: it's there, there is innovation, but not at the same torrid pace and with the same enthusiasm and creative spirit as in newly developing crypto cities.

Zug, Switzerland

Switzerland is the most crypto-friendly place in Europe. It is home to the Ethereum Foundation, along with dozens of other crypto foundations, including Cardano, Tezos, and Cosmos. Early on, Zug, Switzerland, was dubbed Crypto Valley for its crypto-friendly laws and history of innovation in fintech. So far, the country has licensed two crypto banks, a crypto assets fund, and a crypto stock exchange. Naturally, since Switzerland has always been a major capital for finance and banking, their banking laws and infrastructure are top of the line and welcoming toward crypto innovation. They are designed to attract business and investment of all kinds.

But if this is where you land, be prepared to pay out the nose. Switzerland is the most expensive country in Western Europe and the third most expensive country in the world. Not to mention, depending on where you're from and what kind of assets you have for starting a business, getting a visa to live and conduct business in the country may be your first hurdle.

Spain and Germany are also following Switzerland's lead, introducing legislation to make starting blockchain companies and trading crypto easier and more accessible.

Malta also gets a lot of recognition as another ideal place for starting a blockchain or crypto company in Europe, for similar reasons to Switzerland. It has been called the world's first crypto island.[40] Binance inaugurated their company in Malta, though there are a lot of arguments that they don't actually operate there. Even so, a number of other exchanges have set up shop there. Malta has also introduced several bills that make clear the legality of crypto in the country, even going so far as establishing a commission of tech experts, the Malta Digital Innovation Authority, to review the licensing of new blockchain businesses and ensure that new projects are legitimate. Prime Minister Joseph Muscat has made it clear that he wants Malta to be on the front line of blockchain. As for lifestyle, living on an island in Med can't be too bad, right?

Cape Town, South Africa

South Africa is growing as a crypto hot spot. You can find bitcoin ATMs in most cities. The Swiss investment firm Crypto Valley Venture Capital recently opened an office in Cape Town, hoping to find the next big start-ups in the region. Cape Town, Durban, and Johannesburg are all attractive choices for expats. Add beautiful beaches, a warm climate, and vibrant culture to the mix, and you've got a recipe for good living. That said, the tax laws here are not necessarily crypto-friendly. The government is cracking down on how cryptos are taxed. They take a number of factors into consideration, but the difference between having your crypto gains taxed as capital (18 percent) versus revenue (45 percent) can really add up.[41]

---

40 Stefan Stankovic, "The 3 Best Places in Europe to Start a Blockchain Company," *Crypto Briefing*, August 30, 2018, https://cryptobriefing.com/best-places-europe-blockchain-startup.

41 "Taxing Crypto Assets at 45% in South Africa—What You Should Know," *BusinessTech*, August 9, 2021, https://businesstech.co.za/news/banking/511006/taxing-crypto-assets-at-45-in-south-africa-what-you-should-know/.

It is early in the timeline, but I would not be surprised if some of the major African metropolises become crypto hubs. Many countries suffer from lack of infrastructure and hyperinflation, which makes it ripe territory for blockchain and crypto projects to offer solutions. Bitcoin and crypto in general are hugely popular across Africa. The continent has the highest adoption rate for crypto in the world, having grown 1,200 percent in the last year.[42] A lot of cities have bitcoin ATMs and thriving crypto trade. Some African countries have also introduced their own CBDCs, like the eDinar in Tunisia and the eNaira in Nigeria. There are dozens of crypto exchanges, even popular crypto influencers across the continent. That said, crypto still has dubious legal status in many countries.

Dubai, United Arab Emirates

To say Dubai (and the UAE in general) is crypto-friendly is probably an understatement. They are doing everything they can to attract blockchain and crypto businesses. In April 2021, they launched the DMCC Crypto Centre, which provides services to help blockchain and crypto businesses. The center offers coworking spaces for blockchain entrepreneurs as well as incubator and accelerator programs for start-ups. The government has also introduced its own CBDC, emCash. And the emirate holds an annual event called Crypto Expo Dubai that explores the latest trends in crypto and hosts some big names in the space. And, obviously, they have massive sovereign wealth funds with capital to deploy for new projects. It is a good place if you have a lot of money to live and work—and you don't mind the heat!

---

42 "Introducing CV VC's Africa Week," *Medium*, November 5, 2021, https://www.cvvc.com/blogs/introducing-cv-vcs-africa-week.

Singapore

Most places across Asia are crypto-friendly, but the best place to be as a developer, innovator, or investor is probably Singapore. Crypto is considered legal property (not tender) and is regulated by the Monetary Authority of Singapore. And it is a pretty friendly regulatory environment. Singapore does not tax capital gains on crypto (with the exception of stablecoins that are pegged to fiat currency), which is a definite advantage. Many start-ups base their blockchain projects out of Singapore, especially Chinese companies. And Singapore is clean, friendly, and temperate. You just have to get over paying fifteen dollars for a beer.

Still, there are a number of cities in Asia that are also major hubs for blockchain development. Seoul, Tokyo, Japan, and Hong Kong are all historically tied to business and global finance and have up-and-coming crypto communities. Even places like Vietnam and Cambodia are getting into the game. And there, your cost of living would be more affordable than in places like Tokyo and Singapore.

Countries Cracking Down on Crypto

Several countries have tried to ban or partially ban crypto, but often the advisories or regulations are unclear and put traders and developers in a legal gray area.

Take China, for example: They have a love-hate relationship with Bitcoin. I won't go into too much detail here because we did a pretty deep dive on China in the chapter on CBDCs, but let me say this: China is a real competitor in the technology sector, and they are not going to want to lose that foothold. Even if they push out cryptocurrencies other than their own CBDC, it looks like they are going to keep developing crypto-less blockchain solutions. The Communist Party's most recent five-year plan for 2021–2025 explicitly includes blockchain and cryptocurrency, including solutions for industries ranging from law enforcement to energy to urban planning.[43] But the basic issue comes down to how the government can regulate and centralize what is essentially a decentralized technology.

India is another place that has "banned" crypto multiple times, but they are also forward thinking about regulating it. So, for now, you can use crypto in India, but it is somewhat ambiguous what the legal or tax situation is or will be going forward. As the second biggest country in the world by population, and one with a rapidly growing economy, India is definitely one to watch. I have talked to Indian entrepreneurs who say despite government overtures, India is a pretty good place to build crypto businesses.

Nigeria is another interesting case. The Nigerian economy relies heavily on remittances, money sent home from Nigerians working abroad. But the steep cost of wire transfers or other traditional means of sending money across borders has meant that Nigerians are looking for better, cheaper, faster alternatives. You guessed it: cryptocurrencies. It doesn't get better, cheaper, or faster than secure peer-to-peer payments through crypto, which is probably why Nigeria is the second largest bitcoin market after the United States.

Nigeria recently launched its own CBDC, the eNaira. It also banned banking institutions from making crypto transactions in February 2021, though the ban hasn't had much impact on actual use and trade of crypto for individuals. Despite the high volume of crypto being traded there, it is probably not a top spot for relocation given the high unemployment, lack of infrastructure, and uncertain legality of crypto.

---

43 Alice Elkman, "China's Blockchain and Cryptocurrency Ambitions," European Union Institute for Security Studies, July 13, 2021, https://www.iss.europa.eu/content/chinas-blockchain-and-cryptocurrency-ambitions.

The fact is that governments recognize there is vast money in crypto and virtually endless potential in blockchain technology. I think they understand that if you can't beat 'em, join 'em. In other words, it is better to tax and regulate than to outright ban crypto, which is hard to implement and enforce anyway. Many of these "anti-crypto" countries are just looking for ways to integrate the tech into their society.

No matter where you are in the world, there is probably a city within five hundred miles of you that is embracing this new technology. There are people and companies innovating to use blockchain to solve real-world problems. Eventually every country is going to have its own crypto capital, and you could be a part of building it. Blockchain and crypto are the future of finance, the internet, commerce—of the world, really.

Now that we have taken a grand tour of some of the places you might base yourself to work in the crypto world, let's talk about what you might *do* in the space. Next up, we will look at different blockchain career paths and discuss what it feels like to work in such a new, volatile, and rapidly growing industry.

> **No matter where you are in the world, there is probably a city within five hundred miles of you that is embracing this new technology.**

CHAPTER 14
CRYPTO CAREERS

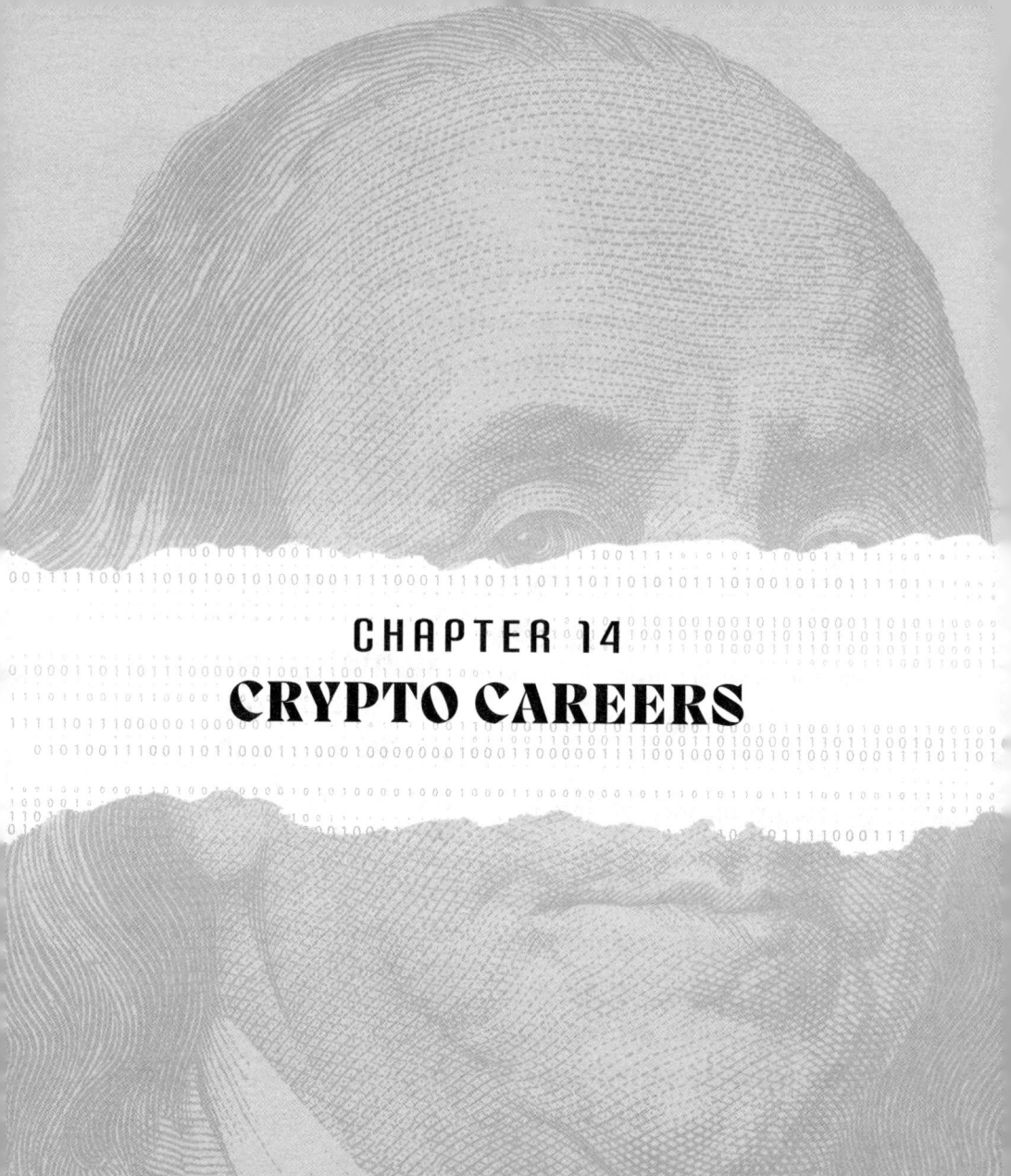

We have come a long way in our discussion of blockchain and crypto, and there is just one more thing I want to talk about with you. In this final chapter, we will learn about some of the many career paths blockchain is opening up and what it feels like to work in the industry. Most people first learn about crypto from the trading or investing side of it, and they want to get involved based on how much money they can make. I am a trader, too, and that is part of what makes crypto exciting. But I also work as a consultant and podcast host helping to bridge the knowledge gap and educate people on how much more blockchain has to offer. I get to work with a diverse group of people, from small businesses to students to developers, and I get to connect people with needs with people with skills.

Everyone I have asked—and I've asked this question a lot—has the same take on why they started working in the industry: It's fun. Working in blockchain and crypto is exciting because you just don't know where it is going. All you know is that *it's going*.

Because of its recent and rapid growth, there are endless opportunities in the industry. Many of the jobs can be done remotely (which is a real perk), and in general, you can make very good money doing them. People in the crypto industry tended to do well during the pandemic. If anything, the industry was bolstered by the fact that people were forced to stay at home and work remotely. So what are the main areas of job growth in blockchain?

Blockchain Developer/Engineer

Job growth in blockchain technology is exponential; its demand is higher than machine learning, artificial intelligence, and UX/UI design. Blockchain is leading the industry in terms of demand for developers. This, of course, has prompted a rush of developers trying to learn the language, the space, the lingo, and all the technical stuff around NFTs, tokenization, and the like. So there is a big market for computer science grads and programmers who are fluent in Python, C++, SQL, and other coding languages.

Even among traditional companies, there is demand for developers skilled in crypto; Amazon, Google, Microsoft—all the big names in tech are actively recruiting for these positions. And the supply is well short of that demand. This means that the financial remuneration tends to be quite substantial. The average salary in the United States for a blockchain developer is $150,000 to $175,000; even beginning developers are looking at six-figure salaries.[44]

In this role, you might be designing the security protocols, developing smart contracts, or creating new apps for a blockchain. Developers also perform routine tasks like analysis, testing, and software debugging. A big draw to this side of the industry is that being a developer in the blockchain space offers the unique challenge of

---

44   Gregory McCubbin, "Blockchain Developer Salary: What Do They Really Earn?" Dapp University, December 22, 2021, https://www.dappuniversity.com/articles/blockchain-developer-salary.

working with decentralized systems—as opposed to traditional IT programmers who work with Web 2.0—which makes it a great option for people who like to think outside the box. The space is abundant with opportunities if you know how to code.

Systems Architect

The design of a blockchain ecosystem—how tokens work, how blockchains interact with each other, how smart contracts operate—is critical to its success and functionality. A systems architect designs how computer systems work. It is similar to the developer role but with more of a big picture feel. It tends to be considered a leadership position within blockchain companies.

As a systems architect, you might be working on cloud computing or building the backbone for various software. It involves determining best practices for your developers, establishing performance metrics for your blockchain, and designing integration architecture for your blockchain to work with other blockchains, apps, or digital services. In other words, you are responsible for decision-making on implementation, operations, and maintenance.

While experienced systems architects will see similar average salary figures as blockchain developers, starting salaries in this field are much more conservative, beginning at just upward of $30,000 a year.[45]

---

45 Toshendra Kumar Sharma, "Blockchain Career Path with Salaries: A Complete Guide," Blockchain Council, https://www.blockchain-council.org/blockchain/blockchain-career-path-with-salaries-a-complete-guide/.

Investor/Entrepreneur

Buying crypto is often the stepping-stone into the wider industry. Most people consider themselves to be investors when they buy bitcoin or some other token, and I would agree with that sentiment. But even if your involvement never goes beyond investing, that can become a career in its own right.

For entrepreneurs, we are in a golden age. You can start a business with little capital because you have access to an ungodly amount of tools and resources, especially if you live in the developed world. It is easy to set up a business and get started, particularly because you do not need the kind of brick-and-mortar investments of a traditional small business. There is little overhead for a crypto investor. All you need is a halfway decent computer or smartphone. And unlike in the olden days of bootstrapping something for years and years, investors in this space can see significant profits in a short period of time.

Every day we are seeing new start-ups in the space, new wallets, new NFT collections, new blockchains and tokens. It is truly never ending. And it's hard even for someone like me to stay up to date with all of that growth. There are just *so many* new businesses being built.

Entrepreneurship isn't limited to investing. You can start something in every facet of the industry. Start your own developer company, your own media or education company, your own NFT or digital art collection, start an agency, build a DAO, or found a legal consultancy. Whatever your interest or expertise, pretty much anything goes because blockchain already ties into everything we do in life.

Trader

Trading is one of those things people think you have to study or spend years cultivating the skill or take a day-trading FOREX master class. The reality is that it *is* a difficult job to take on as a beginner. It does not matter how intelligent or educated you are; if you are not good at it, that is that. The converse side is that if you're good, you're good. I think people either have a natural knack for trading or they don't. It is more than numbers, analytics, technical analysis, risk management—the kinds of things you might learn from a book or tutorial. Trading is as much art as science. Instinct as well as information.

Markets are driven by psychology more than anything, so if you understand human behavior, you can begin to discern and dissect patterns in the market, and that is what will help you excel as a trader. Sure, numbers and analytics are useful tools, but they can't accurately quantify the totality of human behavior. Human psychology is messy, unpredictable, and often irrational.

I got into trading when I saw this frantic 24-7 global market, and I dove in. I lost money, did poorly for a while, lost some more money, lost still more, but then I finally got better and figured out what works for me. There are thousands of studies, metrics, and indicators you can use. I found the ones I like and devised a trading strategy that works for me and my life. That is really what it comes down to. If you love staring at numbers and charts every day and can measure or deconstruct it for yourself, then you can do well and make great money trading. Then there is no limit.

But trading is also a volatile pursuit. You have to be willing to lose as well as gain. That's the two-sided nature of it. That means you have to have a strong stomach because you are going to lose eventually and sometimes lose big. If you can't bear that (financially or emotionally), if you lack reliable risk management skills, or if you don't know when to step away or make a change or accept you're wrong, you will get hammered. It's not unlike gambling in terms of mindset. You can be a skilled card player, but your own mind can trick you into making bad decisions. Trading is as much about emotion as intellect.

I don't recommend it as a profession unless you love it. It is stressful and tiring looking at a screen all day, trying to parse every little tick and bar. It is not a hobby, and it is *definitely not* a get rich quick scheme.

Personally, I love it. I love the thrill. But I have my limits and know how much I'm willing to lose. I know when to walk away from the table, so to speak.

The best way to get your feet wet is take some amount of money that you would be okay losing and give it a shot. Try your hand and see what happens. If you can turn a little bit of money into more money, manage your losses and gains well, you just might get rich. Then again, you can place a trade, go to the kitchen to make a sandwich, and come back to find that you're already down 20 percent. It's happened to me.

And Anything Else You Can Imagine ...

If I haven't said it enough already, blockchain is revolutionizing the way we do everything. Absolutely everything. That means there are going to be opportunities in blockchain for nearly every industry and every skill set. We will need project and operations managers, legal consultants, UX/UI designers, sales and marketing teams, financial advisors, professional writers for white papers—whatever your skill set and experience, there is likely a position in the blockchain world ready and waiting for you. If you're an artist, you might look at creating an NFT collection. If you are into gaming and game development, you can explore opportunities for creating in-game tokens and other blockchain extensions.

And don't think that you need a long résumé of experience and achievements. You don't need a college education to succeed in this industry; you just need the skills. One of the other things I love about crypto is the opportunity it gives people to pivot. Sometimes you meet people who were working at Burger King last year and now they are a leading architect with Polygon, or they are living abroad and doing education and outreach for the Ethereum Foundation. I mean, that is basically what I did. Yes, I completed my bachelor's degree in neuroscience and was bound for medical school, but I realized that was not the path best suited for me, and I bailed. I was able to apply my degree to trading and understand markets. But it wouldn't have happened if I didn't pivot and find something that truly excited me.

> **Blockchain is revolutionizing the way we do everything. Absolutely everything.**

The takeaway here is that the sky is the limit. Just use your imagination!

Riding the Wave

So let's imagine you have found your perfect career niche in the blockchain community. What is it like to work in the industry?

For me and for most of the experts and creators I've interviewed, it is a huge dopamine rush. It is an exciting industry; there is always something going on. And it can also be a highly collaborative community space. Innovation doesn't happen in a vacuum. Yes, many of these blockchains are in competition with each other, but they are also building on each other's advances and solutions. And they all gain by the success and wider adoption of the technology.

I would also say it does differ qualitatively from working in traditional tech spaces—even those with cutting-edge applications. Take artificial intelligence, for example. Every major tech company probably has an AI division. Apple has Siri, Microsoft has Cortana, Amazon has Alexa—you get the picture. Everyone wants to build an amazing AI to help with your everyday life. And it is a cool, interesting, growing industry, but it lacks the Wild West drama of crypto, with its changing regulatory landscape, high-profile hacks, and headline-making achievements. Working in tech, I don't doubt you can find ways to make your work feel fresh and innovative, but the industry as a whole is established and, frankly, corporate. (I mean, does anyone who has seen Mark Zuckerberg in his Facebook Metaverse ad pretending to eat toast like a human really want to work in that space?) And that staleness, to me, blunts its *excitement*.

Crypto, on the other hand, is an unexplored frontier. There is always breaking news, drama, interesting people, a new wave or trend, or the next big thing. Crypto has taken the world by storm. That is not going to stop any time soon.

Crypto has taken the world by storm. That is not going to stop any time soon.

I love waking up and feeling energized by what I do. It is easy for even interesting careers to get boring or repetitive. Blockchain makes life a little more fun. And there's a *movement* behind it; it stands for something: fighting back against corrupt governments, corporations, and big banks to give power back to the people. It is thrilling to be a part of something and feel like you are making a difference (and make good money while doing it).

You can never get bored doing it. I know I haven't.

CONCLUSION
WHAT'S NEXT FOR BLOCKCHAIN?

We have covered tremendous ground together. One of the challenges of writing this book is that there is so much going on in this industry. Even as I was writing chapters, new stories would break related to what I was writing about. And that's a good thing. It goes to show just how thrilling and evergreen the space is. Despite the breadth and depth of what we have discussed—bitcoins, altcoins, stablecoins, digital currencies, NFTs, and DeFi—it would be impossible to keep track of everything that's happening because the space is growing so fast and making inroads into so many industries, sectors, and communities. That testifies to how cool and innovative blockchain technology is, how bright of a future it has, and how much crypto will mold *our* future.

The technology that blockchain resembles most is the early internet. Many have made this comparison and rightfully so. When the internet first emerged, some dismissed it as a passing trend. Most could not understand it or what it might do. And obviously the internet has become one of the most important technologies in history. We don't think about it as a technological apparatus separate from our daily lives, we don't think about how Google or Microsoft works, we don't care about the backbone of the internet. People care about what it can do for them and how they can use it to improve their everyday lives.

I expect blockchain will follow a similar course, from something you see in the news to something that is just *there*, ubiquitous, integrated with virtually everything we do. Not only can it help change each industry, but it will change the internet itself. With the exception of Bitcoin, the remainder of the blockchain space—that is, the majority of the industry—has only been around for six or seven years. That's it. It is still maturing. So it's an exciting time as mainstream adoption takes hold. I am confident that in ten or twenty years, blockchain and crypto will be fully integrated into society. Just like the internet.

Let's be honest, most people don't care about the details of white papers, if they read them at all. In the future, everyone will simply *use* blockchain each day. We won't be concerned about how it works, how smart contracts are executed, or the technical ins and outs any more than we are concerned about how our smartphones work or a pencil gets made. You just want to push a button and reap a benefit, and in the case of blockchain, it helps that the technology makes things better, faster, cheaper, and more secure. Blockchain will make the internet, manufacturing, logistics and supply chains, retail, the food industry—you name it—better a thousand times over. Next thing you know, you will hear about how you can use blockchain to order and pay at Starbucks, vote for your candidate, and track the rollout of the next COVID-19 vaccine. Because it *does* work, and it makes your life better.

Crypto is already a trillion-dollar sector, which wasn't true of the internet six or seven years into its creation. Sure, people made a lot of money during the dot-com boom, but the crypto industry is already well on the way to maturity, even though it is still really in its infancy.

In a few years, it'll be a multitrillion-dollar industry, and Bitcoin will be a trillion-dollar asset in and of itself.

The aim of this book was to give you a glimpse into blockchain but more importantly to ignite your enthusiasm, to make you as passionate and optimistic about it as I am. I hope having read this, you will get on board as blockchain reshapes and improves our world. The revolution is unfolding now. Many people will miss it. Some won't, and they'll benefit tremendously.

> **In the future, everyone will simply *use* blockchain each day.**

So get out there. Get a blockchain job. Buy some tokens. Become a developer. Found a start-up. Launch a new exchange or token. Start thinking about how you can integrate blockchain into your own business or personal life.

I will continue sharing all this stuff in my other projects and ventures with an eye toward uncovering the next big opportunities. And I will continue sharing outside the book so that you can keep up with me personally, continue learning, and keep stoking your excitement. Crypto is not just a technology or a sector but a giant community interconnecting a lot of people in a lot of places under a common, noble aim: a more decentralized future, more power to the people, and greater individual freedoms.

I have seen crypto bring people with very different viewpoints together, people who would never otherwise interact with each other. Left and right wing, minimalist and materialist, underprivileged and wealthy. Blockchain helps people shed their biases and unites us in the service of a common goal. It is the most democratic technology out there, with a lot of promise. So dive in and be a part of the future of blockchain.

What's Next for *BlockHash*?

I'm thrilled to have taken this journey down the blockchain rabbit hole with you. I love being in this community and sharing what I know with other people—whether you are a CEO, an entrepreneur, a Redditor, or just curious about the space. One of the main ways I get to do that is through my podcast, *BlockHash*. Podcasting is one of the most fun things I have ever done because I've met so many cool people, and it has opened many doors for me.

Now we're evolving the podcast into a full-blown show. We are exploring adding in augmented and virtual reality features and translating the content into multiple languages. I can envision a dedicated streaming or TV channel about blockchain where twenty-four hours a day you could tune into amazing, professionally produced programming. Meanwhile, I would like to build some kind of educational content channel; whether that ends up as a Netflix series or book series, I don't yet know. And I think it would be cool to establish an actual physical location—a center of learning where people could come from all over the world and exchange ideas or learn the skills needed to be fluent in the blockchain world. And I certainly hope to keep this content free so that people can enjoy it without having to open their wallets. I just want people to feel a part of this space. You can check it out at blockhashpodcast.com if you haven't already.

My consulting business by the same name is also evolving into a bigger, more successful company. (As a side note, my dog is my company mascot.) It is currently headquartered in Colombia, rechristened as Blocolombia. We hope we will technologically revolutionize Colombia and, eventually, other markets in Latin America. We are working with local governments and small and medium businesses to facilitate the shift toward blockchain, adapting the technology, and helping them understand how it can help them fulfill their mission.

And, ultimately, I think it will make Colombia more prosperous, free, and democratic. I envision Blocolombia being the go-to consultancy for blockchain in the region and perhaps beyond. And I really hope to help Colombia become one of the big breakout countries in the space, to put Colombia on the crypto map.

I intend to remain in Medellín for the foreseeable future. I love living here, and there's a lot of opportunity here. As there is in other emerging, "second world" economies. They're in the best position to lead the charge into the future. I expect Latin America, Africa, and Asia will thrive as crypto leaders in the next few decades. I'm excited to be front and center for that.

And last but not least, I'm still trading and investing because I love it. And who knows what offer might pop up on the radar tomorrow?

If you want to keep up with me directly and follow what I'm up to, you can sign up for my weekly newsletter. It's $250 per month, which believe it or not is on the cheaper end for such newsletters. It is incredibly beneficial, especially if you've enjoyed the book. It will help you stay informed and up to date, and it is an entryway into the wider community and its many opportunities. There is also a condensed, free version. The free version is basically a taste of what is in the paid edition. The paid one has a lot of my personal insights and opinions regarding what's happening in the industry, updated on a weekly basis. I cover a ton of material that's not in the mainstream news and not on the podcast. I also offer insights as a trader, looking at the market, breaking down trades, analysis, applying my own metrics and methods to gauge the markets and make calls (though I'm not a financial advisor, just offering my educated opinion). It talks about the next big opportunities—select, obscure niches that are worth knowing about before the crowd—in decentralized banking, DAOs, NFTs, everything you can think of, *plus* the things you aren't thinking about because you don't know about them yet! So you can sign up for the free one and then, if you like it, subscribe to the premium version.

And of course you can stay engaged with me through social media. Follow me on Twitter @zempcapital and Instagram @zempcapital and @theblockhash.

A Final Thought

Blockchain is more than just a cool technology. It is a special moment in our history as a species. Totally unprecedented. It is a technology that stands to change *all* technologies and alter life, society, and government in a time when the world is facing so many simultaneous, cascading crises. It may not be a panacea, but blockchain will go a long way toward making the world much better, in myriad ways. And we are fortunate to be involved in the early stages. It is going to change the world, and you don't want to miss that. This is the scene in *Independence Day* when everyone, everywhere in the world, is suiting up for battle.

It may not be a panacea, but blockchain will go a long way toward making the world much better, in myriad ways.

Even if you are not invested in it or building a business, just take a step back and appreciate how wondrous the technology is and how it can and will revolutionize everything. One day we'll look back at 2021 and 2022 and 2023 as some of the most important years technologically speaking in our evolution. It will change our lives and those of our children and grandchildren, who will know nothing except a world made better by blockchain.

It's a special time, worthy of reflection. And I myself am deeply honored to be part of this industry and this global movement and community. I encourage people to take a look, even if you're skeptical, even if you don't like it—just take a second look. Opportunities like this don't come around often. Blockchain is a once in a millennium technology.

And it's fascinating to think that the person who invented it remains completely anonymous to this day. That's unbelievably amazing—we've been given this incredible gift by someone we don't even know, who evidently wants no credit or publicity for his contribution. I take a step back and ponder the magnitude of this once in a while. It is an incredible legacy, and hopefully, for you, it's also a starting point.

ACKNOWLEDGMENTS

Thank you to every guest that has appeared on the podcast. I started my journey podcasting with the goal of sharing great conversations about the blockchain industry, and in turn I learned more about the technology myself. It has been an invaluable experience and something that has allowed me to build a solid career.

A massive thank you goes out to my followers and subscribers. Without you, I wouldn't be where I am now. I hope to share more with you all on my journey through life as I tackle new and exciting challenges around blockchain and crypto. I also hope to expand quickly into the Spanish-speaking world and reach a wider audience, making more of what I do inclusive to more people.

To my friends and family, I appreciate the support on this bold journey publishing another book. It's been long and stressful, but I'm thrilled to share this adventure with the people closest to me.

# ABOUT THE AUTHOR

Brandon Zemp is a twenty-eight-year-old entrepreneur and investor who graduated with his neuroscience degree from Pitzer College in Claremont, California. His initial direction was medical school, but he decided to pivot and travel after college. Not too long after, he began to apply his knowledge to trade strategy, economics, and developing blockchain-based solutions.

He made his mark early on as a trader in the fast-paced crypto market. Shortly after, he established his first company, BlockHash LLC, a blockchain consultancy providing educational resources for small business owners, students, developers, and investors. This has been accomplished through his popular show, *BlockHash: Exploring the Blockchain*, and his weekly newsletter, the *BlockHash Insider*.

He currently lives in Medellín, Colombia, where he has started another company called Blocolombia, another blockchain consultancy that is focused on educating and integrating blockchain in both the public sector and private sector. Their mission is to help build a smarter future for Colombia with blockchain technology and begin evolving the country as a whole.

Brandon is also working on additional endeavors, including the world's first podcast NFT collection, where each NFT represents a specific episode and can be purchased to gain a sponsorship placement on the show. Brandon believes that the future of the NFT space will be less speculative and more utility driven. The podcast NFT collection will help serve as a powerful use case to define how NFTs can be applied in the future economy.